OTHELLO

NOTES

including
- *Life of Shakespeare*
- *Brief Synopsis of the Play*
- *List of Characters*
- *Summaries & Commentaries*
- *Character Analyses*
- *Questions for Review*
- *Selected Bibliography*

by
Gary Carey, M.A.
University of Colorado

INCORPORATED

LINCOLN, NEBRASKA 68501

Editor	Consulting Editor
Gary Carey, M.A. *University of Colorado*	*James L. Roberts, Ph.D.* *Department of English* *University of Nebraska*

ISBN 0-8220-0063-6
© Copyright 1980
by
C. K. Hillegass
All Rights Reserved
Printed in U.S.A.

1993 Printing

Cliffs Notes, Inc.   Lincoln, Nebraska

CONTENTS

OTHELLO

Notes

LIFE OF SHAKESPEARE

Many books have assembled facts, reasonable suppositions, tradi-
tions, and speculations concerning the life and career of William
Shakespeare. Taken as a whole, these materials give a rather com-
prehensive picture of England's foremost dramatic poet. Tradition and
sober supposition are not necessarily false because they lack proved
bases for their existence. It is important, however, that persons interested in Shakespeare should distinguish between *facts* and *beliefs*
about his life.

From one point of view, modern scholars are fortunate to know
as much as they do about a man of middle-class origin who left a small
English country town and embarked on a professional career in
sixteenth-century London. From another point of view, they know
surprisingly little about the writer who has continued to influence
the English language and its drama and poetry for more than three
hundred years. Sparse and scattered as these facts of his life are, they
are sufficient to prove that a man from Stratford by the name of
William Shakespeare wrote the major portion of the thirty-seven plays
which scholars ascribe to him. The concise review which follows will
concern itself with some of these records.

No one knows the exact date of William Shakespeare's birth. His
baptism occurred on Wednesday, April 26, 1564. His father was John
Shakespeare, tanner, glover, dealer in grain, and town official of Stratford; his mother, Mary, was the daughter of Robert Arden, a pros-
perous gentleman-farmer. The Shakespeares lived on Henley Street.

Under a bond dated November 28, 1582, William Shakespeare
and Anne Hathaway entered into a marriage contract. The baptism
of their eldest child, Susanna, took place in Stratford in May, 1583.

One year and nine months later their twins, Hamnet and Judith, were christened in the same church. The parents named them for the poet's friends Hamnet and Judith Sadler.

Early in 1596, William Shakespeare, in his father's name, applied to the College of Heralds for a coat of arms. Although positive proof is lacking, there is reason to believe that the Heralds granted this request, for in 1599 Shakespeare again made application for the right to quarter his coat of arms with that of his mother. Entitled to her father's coat of arms, Mary had lost this privilege when she married John Shakespeare before he held the official status of gentleman.

In May of 1597, Shakespeare purchased New Place, the outstanding residential property in Stratford at that time. Since John Shakespeare had suffered financial reverses prior to this date, William must have achieved success for himself.

Court records show that in 1601 or 1602, William Shakespeare began rooming in the household of Christopher Mountjoy in London. Subsequent disputes between Shakespeare's landlord, Mountjoy, and his son-in-law, Stephen Belott, over Stephen's wedding settlement led to a series of legal actions, and in 1612 the court scribe recorded Shakespeare's deposition of testimony relating to the case.

In July, 1605, William Shakespeare paid four hundred and forty pounds for the lease of a large portion of the tithes on certain real estate in and near Stratford. This was an arrangement whereby Shakespeare purchased half the annual tithes, or taxes, on certain agricultural products from sections of land in and near Stratford. In addition to receiving approximately ten percent income on his investment, he almost doubled his capital. This was possibly the most important and successful investment of his lifetime, and it paid a steady income for many years.

Shakespeare is next mentioned when John Combe, a resident of Stratford, died on July 12, 1614. To his friend, Combe bequeathed the sum of five pounds. These records and similar ones are important, not because of their economic significance but because they prove the existence of a William Shakespeare in Stratford and in London during this period.

On March 25, 1616, William Shakespeare revised his last will and testament. He died on April 23 of the same year. His body lies within the chancel and before the altar of the Stratford church. A rather wry inscription is carved upon his tombstone:

Good Friend, for Jesus' sake, forbear
To dig the dust enclosed here;
Blest be the man that spares these stones
And curst be he that moves my bones.

The last direct descendant of William Shakespeare was his grand-daughter, Elizabeth Hall, who died in 1670.

These are the most outstanding facts about Shakespeare the man, as apart from those about the dramatist and poet. Such pieces of information, scattered from 1564 through 1616, declare the existence of such a person, not as a writer or actor, but as a private citizen. It is illogical to think that anyone would or could have fabricated these details for the purpose of deceiving later generations.

In similar fashion, the evidence establishing William Shakespeare as the foremost playwright of his day is positive and persuasive. Robert Greene's *Groatsworth of Wit*, in which he attacked Shakespeare, a mere actor, for presuming to write plays in competition with Greene and his fellow playwrights, was entered in the *Stationers' Register* on September 20, 1592. In 1594 Shakespeare acted before Queen Elizabeth, and in 1594 and 1595 his name appeared as one of the shareholders of the Lord Chamberlain's Company. Francis Meres in his *Palladis Tamia* (1598) called Shakespeare "mellifluous and hony-tongued" and compared his comedies and tragedies with those of Plautus and Seneca in excellence.

Shakespeare's continued association with Burbage's company is equally definite. His name appears as one of the owners of the Globe in 1599. On May 19, 1603, he and his fellow actors received a patent from James I designating them as the King's Men and making them Grooms of the Chamber. Late in 1608 or early in 1609, Shakespeare and his colleagues purchased the Blackfriars Theatre and began using it as their winter location when weather made production at the Globe inconvenient.

Other specific allusions to Shakespeare, to his acting and his writing, occur in numerous places. Put together, they form irrefutable testimony that William Shakespeare of Stratford and London was the leader among Elizabethan playwrights.

One of the most impressive of all proofs of Shakespeare's authorship of his plays is the First Folio of 1623, with the dedicatory verse which appeared in it. John Heminge and Henry Condell, members of Shakespeare's own company, stated that they collected and issued the plays as a memorial to their fellow actor. Many contemporary poets contributed eulogies to Shakespeare; one of the best known of these poems is by Ben Jonson, a fellow actor and, later, a friendly rival. Jonson also criticized Shakespeare's dramatic work in *Timber: or, Discoveries* (1641).

Certainly there are many things about Shakespeare's genius and career which the most diligent scholars do not know and cannot explain, but the facts which do exist are sufficient to establish Shakespeare's identity as a man and his authorship of the thirty-seven plays which reputable critics acknowledge to be his.

BRIEF SYNOPSIS OF THE PLAY

Othello opens in the great and powerful city-state of Venice. It is late at night. Roderigo, a young gentleman and former suitor of Senator Brabantio's daughter, Desdemona, is angry with Iago, a soldier in the Venetian army. Iago knew about Desdemona's elopement with the leader of the Venetian forces, a Moor named Othello, yet, complains Roderigo, Iago did not tell him. Roderigo reminds Iago that he has said that he hates the Moor, and if this is so, why did he not report Othello's conquest of Desdemona to Roderigo immediately? Iago is defensively adamant: he hates Othello, and he is burning with jealousy that he, Iago, has been passed over for a promotion. For years, Iago has been Othello's faithful ensign and he expected to be promoted to the rank of lieutenant; instead, the post went to a young man from Florence, Michael Cassio, whom Iago holds in great contempt because all Cassio knows of soldiering is what he has learned from books. Iago, on the other hand, is a veteran of many hard-fought campaigns. Iago tells Roderigo to awaken Desdemona's father and inform him that his daughter has run off with the Moor.

The two stand before Brabantio's house and call to him. When the senator appears at a window, Iago takes great pleasure in telling him the news. But before the old man comes running down to see exactly what the trouble is, Iago leaves quickly, telling Roderigo that as the Moor's trusted ensign it is not right that he should be involved. He must still pretend love and loyalty to Othello, who is about to embark for Cyprus with the army to fight the Turks.

A distraught Brabantio, with his servants, appears downstairs and demands to know where he can find Othello and his daughter. Roderigo agrees to take him to Othello.

In the next scene, we find Othello with Iago and several attendants on another street. Now Iago is telling Othello about Brabantio's reaction to his daughter's marriage. Iago warns Othello that her father will do whatever he can to take his daughter from the Moor. Cassio then enters to tell Othello that the Duke of Venice has sent for him to come immediately, for there is alarming news from Cyprus. A moment later, the enraged Brabantio bursts upon the scene, along with several armed followers. But Othello will not allow his men to draw their swords against his new father-in-law. Instead, they all agree to appear before the Duke. Brabantio is sure that the Duke will take his side against Othello.

However, the war news is critically urgent, and the Duke, who admires Othello, needs him to lead the Venetian forces. He listens to Othello's story of his newfound love, and then, when Desdemona appears and makes it clear that she now belongs to Othello, the Duke attempts to reconcile Brabantio, Desdemona, and Othello—but to no avail. Brabantio will have no more to do with Desdemona and will not even allow her to remain in his house while Othello is off to war. Desdemona, at this point, speaks up and insists on following her new husband to Cyprus. Othello decides to leave his bride in the care of her maid, Emilia, and Emilia's husband, Iago, Othello's most trusted friend; the Moor and his new bride then go off to spend their last few hours alone together. Iago tells Roderigo not to give up hope for Desdemona; he still may win her, for she will undoubtedly soon tire of the Moor. When Roderigo, somewhat encouraged, leaves, Iago reveals in a soliloquy his deep hatred and jealousy of Othello, and he mulls over a possible way to destroy him. He decides, at last, to use Cassio, the man he deeply resents, as the instrument of his revenge.

The scene of the drama now changes to the island of Cyprus. There has been a great storm at sea which has wrecked the Turkish fleet and held up Othello's arrival. Cassio's ship arrives first, and a short while later Desdemona lands, along with Emilia and Iago. Desdemona is concerned for Othello, and to take her mind off her worries, Cassio engages her in lighthearted conversation. Iago, seeing how well they get on together, visualizes the crystallization of his plan. When the victorious Othello arrives at last and goes off happily with his bride, Iago tells Roderigo that he is convinced that it is really

Cassio whom Desdemona loves. Skillfully, Iago induces Roderigo to pick a quarrel with Cassio that same evening.

Shortly afterward, a herald appears and announces that the night will be given over to feasting and celebration in honor of Othello's victory and, belatedly, as a celebration for the newly married couple.

Later that night, Cassio is left in charge of the night watch while Othello and Desdemona retire to their chambers. Iago plies Cassio with wine and teases him until his mood becomes irritable. Then Roderigo appears, according to plan, and he begins to fight with Cassio. Montano, governor of the island, tries to stop the fight and is wounded by the drunken Cassio.

Othello appears, and when he is told what happened, he removes Cassio from his position as lieutenant. Cassio, now somewhat sobered and deeply sorry for all the trouble, is about to plead with Othello, but Iago quickly persuades him that his chances will be better if he asks Desdemona to intercede for him with her husband. Iago then helps Cassio arrange to meet Desdemona privately, and Desdemona naively promises Cassio that she will do everything she can to restore him to Othello's good graces.

As Cassio is leaving, Iago and Othello appear. Othello notices Cassio's speedy departure, and Iago quickly seizes the opportunity to point out that Cassio seemed to be trying to avoid the Moor. Desdemona immediately and enthusiastically begins to beg Othello to pardon Cassio and will not stop her pleading until Othello agrees.

The moment Desdemona and Emilia leave, however, Iago begins to plant seeds of doubt and suspicion in Othello's mind. Over and over again, all the while pretending to speak plainly and honestly, Iago subtly suggests that Desdemona and Cassio are having a love affair. When Iago is gone, Desdemona returns and finds her formerly gentle and loving husband in an overwrought emotional condition. She tries to soothe him by stroking his head with her handkerchief, but he irritably pushes it aside; it falls to the ground, and he leaves.

A while later, Emilia finds the handkerchief and gives it to Iago. It is a very special handkerchief, embroidered with a strawberry pattern, and was Othello's first present to Desdemona. Then Othello returns, demanding of Iago some proof of his wife's infidelity. The quick-witted Iago, thinking of the handkerchief in his pocket, says that he overheard Cassio talk in his sleep about Desdemona, and that, furthermore, he noticed Cassio wiping his face with a strawberry-embroidered handkerchief. Othello is now convinced that Desdemona has been unfaithful to him. He angrily vows revenge against both Cassio and Desdemona. Impulsively, he also promotes "honest" Iago to be his new lieutenant.

Now Othello cannot wait to ask Desdemona where the handkerchief is, and when she cannot produce it, he flies into a rage of jealousy. Meanwhile, Iago has left the handkerchief where Cassio cannot fail to find it. He then arranges for Othello to actually see the handkerchief in Cassio's possession. Othello and Iago agree that Othello should kill Desdemona; Iago will dispose of Cassio. At that moment, Lodovico arrives from Venice with orders for Othello to return at once, leaving Cassio as Governor of Cyprus. Events move swiftly to a climax as Othello accuses Desdemona of infidelity and refuses to believe her protestations of innocence. He orders her to go to bed.

Iago, meanwhile, persuades the gullible Roderigo to kill Cassio. Later that night, Iago and Roderigo attack Cassio on a dark street. However, things do not work out as Iago planned, for it is Cassio who wounds Roderigo. Iago then rushes out and stabs Cassio in the leg. Othello, hearing Cassio's cries for help, believes that half of the revenge plan is completed, and he hastens to fulfill his own act of revenge. But neither Cassio nor Roderigo is dead, and Iago, fearful that Roderigo will talk, quickly and secretly kills him. Emilia then enters and is sent to tell Othello what happened.

Othello, deaf to Desdemona's pleas and prayers, has smothered her in her bed. Emilia tries to get into the room, but not until he is sure that his wife is dead will Othello unlock the doors and let Emilia enter. Desdemona revives briefly, tries to take the blame from Othello, then dies. Othello then tells Emilia what he has done. Stricken with horror, Emilia tells him that Iago's accusations were all lies, and runs for help. The others enter, and Othello explains why he killed Desdemona. Emilia then tells him that it was she who took the fateful handkerchief and gave it to her husband. Iago stabs and kills his wife and is himself wounded by the Moor, who, remorseful and heartbroken, stabs himself. He dies, falling across Desdemona's body.

LIST OF CHARACTERS

Othello

A Moorish general serving the city-state of Venice. He is a seasoned warrior, an honest man, and a new husband. His flaw is that he allows his ensign's diabolical nature to corrupt him and make him believe that his young wife, Desdemona, is unfaithful. It is only after Othello kills her that he learns that he has been duped. In deep anguish, he executes himself for his crime.

Iago

Othello's ensign, who hoped to be promoted to the position of lieutenant. The position went to Michael Cassio, and Iago vows revenge. He manages to destroy Othello, Desdemona, his own wife (Emilia), and even his Venetian patron, Roderigo. He has often been said to be Shakespeare's most consummate villain.

Desdemona

The daughter of the Venetian Senator Brabantio and the wife of the Venetian General Othello. Against her father's wishes, she marries a foreigner, a Moor – a man of another color and of another race. Her love for Othello is so deep, however, that as she is dying, she attempts to protect him from his crime.

Cassio

Othello's Florentine lieutenant is young and handsome. He is courteous to the ladies and, in order to seem a good soldier and friend to Iago, he drinks too much, wounds Montano, Governor of Cyprus, and is dismissed from his post by Othello. By sheer luck, he manages to escape being killed in a murder plot contrived by Iago. At the end of the play, it is Cassio who is appointed Governor of Cyprus.

Emilia

Iago's wife is outspoken, a bit bawdy, and has a certain cynicism about men – due mainly to years of living with Iago. Despite this, however, even she does not suspect her husband of his labyrinthine web of evil machinations. In one sense, one can say that she is an agent in the death of Desdemona. She has an opportunity to explain to Othello that his wife did not give a sentimentally prized handkerchief to young Cassio, but she remains silent. After Iago stabs Emilia and as she is dying, she finally manages to convince Othello that his wife was faithful.

Roderigo

A Venetian who is deeply enamored with Desdemona. Iago convinces him that if Roderigo will pay him sufficiently, he will arrange, eventually, for Roderigo to have Desdemona.

The Duke of Venice

He appoints Othello to lead the Venetian forces against the Turks and, because of his admiration for the Moor, he tries to placate Brabantio's anger against his daughter and her new husband.

Brabantio

He is a senator of Venice; he is also Desdemona's father and is outraged and heartbroken when he learns of her marriage to the Moor, Othello.

Gratiano

Brabantio's brother, who, together with a kinsman, Lodovico, discovers Cassio lying wounded after he has been attacked by Roderigo.

Montano

Governor of Cyprus; a friend and loyal supporter of Othello.

Clown

Othello's servant; he teases the Cyprian musicians about their instruments, and he serves as a messenger between Cassio and Desdemona.

Bianca

Cassio's jealous mistress; he gives her Desdemona's handkerchief, not realizing whose handkerchief it really is.

Lodovico

Kinsman to Brabantio; he and Gratiano discover Cassio lying wounded after he has been attacked by Roderigo.

SUMMARIES AND COMMENTARIES

ACT I – SCENE 1

Summary

The scene opens late at night on a street in Venice. Iago, an ensign in the Venetian navy, and Roderigo, a wealthy Venetian gentleman, are discussing the recent elopement of Desdemona, a woman Roderigo hoped to marry. Roderigo protests indignantly that he paid Iago good money to keep him informed about Desdemona's romantic attachments and, we infer, to try to kindle a love match between the two. Iago failed, and Desdemona eloped with Iago's general; the fact that Iago did not inform Roderigo immediately seems to prove to Roderigo that Iago's loyalty is really with Othello. In defense, Iago declares that he has no special loyalty toward his general. In fact, he has every reason to hate the man; after all, Othello recently made Cassio, instead of Iago, his new lieutenant. Iago then tells Roderigo that his is a difficult role; to the public, he must seem to be a dutiful servant to Othello, but, in fact, he is seeking his own "peculiar [private] end" (60).

Meanwhile, Iago and Roderigo have reached Desdemona's father's house and decide to wake up her father, Brabantio, and tell him that his daughter has eloped with Othello. Brabantio is understandably furious and demands vengeance, and while Iago slips away on business of his own, Brabantio sets off with Roderigo and a search party to find his missing daughter and Othello.

Commentary

The play begins with two people conversing, establishing theatrical time, place, and situation. This is an often-used theatrical convention, giving us background information and creating curiosity about the main character before he appears onstage. Yet the conversation here is not merely idle chatter. This is a quarrel of sorts and, as such, it serves several functions. Its tone easily catches our interest and, second, it reveals Iago's wily nature; he must make amends to Roderigo for failing to arouse Desdemona's interest in him. After all, Iago intends to keep a hand in this wealthy nobleman's pocketbook, which, Roderigo says, belongs to Iago, "as if the strings were thine" (3). Iago apologizes profusely for failing Roderigo. Never did he dream that such an elopement might occur: "If ever I did dream of such a matter," he says, "Abhor me" (5-6).

Exactly how long Iago has been capitalizing upon the gullibility of Roderigo, this Venetian dandy, we do not know, but it is clear that Iago has no respect for the man's intelligence. The guile he openly uses to stay in Roderigo's good stead is not even particularly crafty; blatantly, for example, he tells Roderigo, "I am not what I am" (65). Besides this statement being a capsule condemnation of Iago, it serves to point out that Roderigo *trusts* this man. Thus Roderigo gains a measure of our pity; he is a weak figure, probably victimized by everybody, not only in this matter of deceit.

Far more important, however, than catching our interest and establishing Iago's basic character, this opening scene sets forth the key elements of the tragedy's conflict—that is, it reveals Iago's deep resentment toward Othello. Iago believed that he would be promoted to the rank of Othello's first lieutenant. He was not. Instead, Othello chose a man whose military ineptitude is an insult to Iago's proven superiority on the battlefield. Iago points out to Roderigo that Cassio, the newly appointed lieutenant, is not a true soldier. He is not even a Venetian. Cassio is a *Florentine*, a damning epithet condemning the city's reputation as being a collection of financiers and bookkeepers. What knowledge Cassio has of the battlefield he gained from textbooks; in other words, he is a student, not a practitioner of battle. Even a spinster, Iago says, knows more of the "division of a battle" (23) than this "bookish theoric" (24). We are inclined to believe Iago, even though we have known him for only a short time. True, he has said, "I am not what I am" (65), but here he states his case concisely and without undue exaggeration. He does seem to be a superior, professional soldier who has had to step aside for a promotion that he feels he deserves. In fact, his candidacy for the position was supported by "three great ones of the city" (8). Iago apparently knows his worth. He has risen through the ranks and has proven his bravery and skill "at Rhodes, at Cyprus, and on other grounds/ Christen'd and heathen" (29-30). He rose through the ranks by sheer ability, hoping for a position next highest to a general and was denied it. He rankles at being Othello's "ancient" — that is, his ensign. Furthermore, there is nothing Iago can do about the situation: "there's no remedy" (35). He realizes that "preferment goes by letter and affection" (36) and not by "old gradation" (37) (the traditional order of society). But he will continue to appear to "serve" Othello, so that eventually he can "serve [his] turn upon him" (42).

Shakespeare makes a strong case for Iago's anger toward Othello and for his motive for revenge. Here we have a clear-cut picture of a man who is professionally wounded; his self-esteem has been insulted and we must, of necessity, realize how deeply he has been offended if we are to understand the full extent of his revenge upon Othello.

Iago, however, is not bent on mere revenge. It would not be an exaggeration to say that revenge *consumes* him, and in this scene he reveals himself to Roderigo, and to us, as a super-egotist, a self-seeking, malicious individual who will use every device in order to attain his "peculiar end" (60).

His first act of revenge is quickly initiated: he will alert and incense Desdemona's father. He tells Roderigo to "call up her father,/ Rouse him. Make after him, poison his delight" (67-68) and make such a noise that it will seem as though "fire/ [has been] spied" (76-77). Roderigo obeys, but Iago is still not satisfied, and he must add *his* strong voice to Roderigo's, crying out loudly four times that "thieves" have plundered Brabantio's home. When Brabantio appears at the window, Iago continues to use the robbery metaphor: "You're robbed," he says, and "have lost half your soul" (85/87).

Here Iago spews forth particularly coarse insults on his general. He calls Othello "an old black ram" (88), referring to the fact that Othello is a Moor, a dark-skinned man; Iago shouts out into the quiet night that this "ram" is "tupping" (88) (copulating with) Brabantio's "white ewe" (89) (Desdemona). He even conjures up another picture of visual horror for the sleepy old gentleman: if Brabantio doesn't rouse the Venetian citizens and rescue Desdemona, "the devil" (91) (another reference to the Moor's soot-colored skin) will make Brabantio a grandfather. The focus here is clearly on Othello's being a demoniac animal – a lust-driven ram raping the pure, white Desdemona. The language is crude and obscene, but one might note here that earlier the seemingly mild-natured Roderigo also made a tasteless reference to Othello as "the thick-lips" (66).

Yet while Iago calls Othello names, he has not yet called him by name; he has referred to him only with damning epithets. Brabantio is still half-asleep, and he has not fully grasped the situation. He is more annoyed that Roderigo has awakened him then he is about the possibility that his house may have been "robbed." Iago's offensive, figurative language has not riled him. We learn that he has warned Roderigo "not to haunt about my doors" (96); "my daughter is not for thee" (98). Thus another dimension of this situation presents itself. Roderigo is not just a rich, lovesick suitor who is paying Iago good wages to further his case with the senator's daughter. Roderigo has been rejected by Brabantio as a candidate for Desdemona's hand – a fact which offers an interesting parallel: Iago has been denied his chance to become Othello's lieutenant, and Roderigo has been denied his chance to become a recognized suitor of Desdemona. Rejection and revenge, then, are doubly potent ingredients in this tragedy.

Iago is quick to realize that the timid Roderigo will never sufficiently raise the ire of Desdemona's father and, for this reason, he interrupts his patron and heaps even more insults on Othello. Yet – and this fact is important – Iago has *still* not named Othello as being the culprit, as being the man who kidnapped Desdemona and eloped with her. This neglect on Iago's part – his failing to identify Othello – is dramatically important. Because Brabantio seems dense and uncomprehending, Iago can continue to curse Othello's so-called villainous nature and, thereby, reveal to us the depths of his own corruptness.

For example, Iago shouts out that Desdemona, at this moment, is being mounted by a "Barbary horse" (112). Brabantio's nephews, he says, will neigh, and, likewise, Brabantio's cousins will be "gennets" (113) (black Spanish horses). Still, however, he has not identified Othello by name; nor does he stress that it is Venice's *General Othello* who has absconded with Brabantio's daughter; Iago's emphasis is on Desdemona's sexual violation and the fact that at this very moment she and the Moor "are [now] making the beast with two backs" (117), a bawdy Elizabethan euphemism for sexual intercourse.

Iago's brazen assertions and Roderigo's timorous apologies for awakening Brabantio are finally effective. Brabantio comprehends what Iago and Roderigo are saying and that they have not been over-indulging in "distemp'ring draughts" (99) of liquor. Coincidentally, Brabantio was having a dream that foretold of just such a calamity. Dreams and omens of this sort are common in literature of this time and create the sense that fate somehow has a hand in the tragic events about to follow. Brabantio calls for "light," as well as for the light of insight to help him understand fully what has happened and how to deal with it. Then, as Brabantio moves into action, calling for more lights and arousing members of his household, Iago steals away, but not before explaining his reasons for doing so: it must not be public knowledge that Iago himself is an enemy of Othello; if Iago's machinations are to be successful, he must outwardly "show out a flag and sign of love,/ Which is indeed but sign" (157-58). Thus he will manage to stay in Othello's good graces. For this reason, he must go and rejoin his general.

In addition to this speech reminding us of Iago's dangerous, diabolical treachery, it also serves to inform us about Othello's significance to Venice. Othello is a superior public figure, one who will soon be summoned to end the Cyprian wars, and a man upon whom the Venetian state depends for its safety. This fact is contained in Iago's comment that "another of his fathom they have none/ To lead their business" (153-54). Othello is a man of high position, as well as one of high honor and one who is, therefore, worthy of being considered a tragic hero.

The subsequent action, in which the distraught and almost incredulous father appears, concludes the scene in an exciting, sustaining manner. Brabantio is pathetic in his nightgown, standing distraught in the light of his servants' torches, realizing that his daughter is indeed gone. His sentences are unfinished, half-thoughts of disbelief. He appeals to fathers everywhere not to trust their daughters' words, only "what you see them act" (172). In his despair, he turns to Roderigo (Desdemona's suitor whom he earlier scorned) for confirmation that perhaps Othello used magic charms to win Desdemona. He is furious with himself for not having allowed Roderigo to court Desdemona. Suddenly Roderigo is ironically elevated to Brabantio's "lieutenant"; Brabantio tells him to "lead on" (181) and to alert every house. Thus

Roderigo and Brabantio's search party sets out for The Sagittary, an inn where Iago said that Othello and Desdemona can be found.

ACT I – SCENE 2

Summary

Shortly afterward, on another street, Iago has just joined Othello, when Cassio delivers a message from the Duke of Venice that summons Othello immediately to a military council. Then, as Brabantio and Roderigo enter, accompanied by armed officers, the scene nearly erupts into violence. Brabantio accuses Othello of having bewitched Desdemona and demands that he be thrown at once into prison. With dignity, Othello manages to pacify the others and persuades Brabantio to take his complaint before the Duke.

Commentary

The first words we hear from Iago in this speech are lies. Posing as the trustworthy, honest soldier, the "loyal ancient" to his general, Iago says that when he inadvertently witnessed Roderigo's rousing Brabantio, he would "nine or ten times . . . have yerk'd [stabbed] him [Roderigo] under the ribs" (4-5); he did not do so only because of his "little godliness" (9) and because of his lack of "iniquity" (3), he says, and because he had not the "very stuff o' th' conscience/ To do no contriv'd murder" (2-3). Iago is a practiced, pathological liar, attributing to Roderigo the "scurvy and provoking terms/ Against [Othello's] honor" (7-8) that he himself proclaimed. Hypocritically, he sighs that it was "full hard [to] forbear him [Roderigo]" (10). This deceitful tone will characterize Iago throughout the play. Just as he earlier pretended great loyalty to Roderigo to continue to fatten his purse, here he pretends full loyalty to Othello, as he will throughout the play. In addition, he feigns overconcern that Brabantio's powerful position in Venice will bring Othello great grief and may dissolve Othello's marriage to Desdemona. Iago is a very versatile villain and wears many masks, in contrast to the commanding integrity of Othello.

Othello answers Iago in just five words, " 'Tis better as it is" (6), he says, meaning that it is good that Iago was not rash in handling Roderigo, for Othello does not fear Brabantio's temper. Our first view of Othello, then, is of a calm man who is in complete control of himself. He does not panic when he hears secondhand information about Roderigo's alleged animosity; nor does he seem to be the "lascivious Moor" (127) that Iago described in the previous scene. Here we will see proof that Othello is a public officer of great importance. "Let him [Brabantio] do his spite," Othello says. "My services . . . shall out-tongue his complaints" (117-19). Although Othello dislikes boasting, he cites the fact that he is no commoner: "I fetch my life and being/ From men of royal siege" (21-22) – that is, he may be black, but he is of royal descent among the Moors, who earlier in history fought their way to the conquest of Spain and made a valiant effort to conquer all of western Europe. And of prime importance in this matter between himself and Brabantio is the fact that he loves "the gentle Desdemona" (25). He speaks with simple and intense feeling for her. He loved his bachelor freedom, but he loved Desdemona more; otherwise, he would not have "confined" his "unhoused free condition" (26), not even for all "the sea's worth" (28).

As he continues to await Desdemona's father, Othello still exhibits neither guilt nor fear. Even when Iago cautions that he sees torches approaching and urges Othello to go within, Othello refuses to hide. He has no apprehension concerning Desdemona's father, nor will he avoid confronting Brabantio's armed party. He is a man confident and prepared: "My parts, my title, and my perfect soul/ Shall manifest me rightly" (31-32). Othello commands our respect and admiration.

Iago's brief acknowledgment of the Moor's character, his swearing softly "by Janus" (33), is almost a throwaway line, one that might go unnoticed, but he could not have selected a more proper or ironical God to swear by, for Janus was the two-faced god of the Romans.

Surprisingly, the party that approaches Othello is not Brabantio's; it is from the Duke of Venice and is led by Cassio, Othello's new Florentine lieutenant, who says that the Duke requires Othello's appearance "haste-post-haste" (37). There is a Turkish threat to the island of Cyprus, an island which is crucial to the defense of Venice. Once more Othello's impeccable and highly regarded reputation is indicated; three search parties have been sent out to find him. It is he who has been singled out, "hotly called for" (44) by the Duke to stop the Turkish uprising and protect Venice.

Furtively, while Othello is gone, Iago tries to whisper to Cassio some news about Othello's elopement, but Othello returns before Iago can begin his gossip. At this point, Brabantio, Roderigo, and their party enter. Swords are drawn, but Othello calmly attempts to reason with Brabantio. He appeals to Brabantio's dignity, that the senator's "years" (60) are more able at commanding than are his "weapons" (61). The grief-stricken father, however, does not listen to Othello's eloquent words of wisdom, and he soundly denounces his unwanted son-in-law. The facts of the elopement are so incredible to him that he is sure that the Moor has used some sort of "foul charms" (73) or even drugs to win Desdemona: "thou hast enchanted her" (63). The marriage seems to be monstrous – in the sense that it represents a deviation from that which is natural. How else, Brabantio asks, would Desdemona, so carefully reared, have brought such scandal upon herself and her father by shunning "the wealthy curled darlings of our nation" (68) and running to the Moor's "sooty bosom" (70)?

Othello continues to remain cool and self-confident when Brabantio orders him arrested and punished. He displays himself as the admirally self-possessed master of the situation. He is willing to answer all of Brabantio's charges, but a prison cell hardly seems the logical place to answer his father-in-law, for the Duke of Venice himself has just now summoned him. Grumbling, Brabantio realizes that he must cease his threats for the present, but he consoles himself with the hope that the Duke and the other senators will surely "feel this wrong as 'twere their own" (97).

ACT I – SCENE 3

Summary

Later the same night, the Duke and his senators, in council, are discussing discrepancies in the several reports about the threatening Turkish fleet. Othello, Brabantio, Iago, Roderigo, and others enter and interrupt this attempt to solve a national crisis. Presenting to them his own personal crisis, Brabantio declares that nothing but witchcraft could have induced his daughter to marry Othello; Othello denies the charge, and the Duke sends attendants to fetch Desdemona, Iago accompanying them at Othello's request. Desdemona is called to speak for herself; in the meanwhile, Othello tells them all how he met and courted his new wife and how he fascinated her with accounts of his travels and adventures. Desdemona arrives and gently resolves the dispute by acknowledging split loyalties to her father and to her new husband, but making it clear that she now belongs to Othello.

Brabantio bitterly rejects his daughter and also the Duke's attempts to console him. The Duke returns his attention to the Turks and directs Othello to leave for Cyprus. Desdemona will join Othello later in Cyprus under Iago's protection. As the others leave, Iago and Roderigo are once again alone. Despite Roderigo's threats of suicide, Iago revitalizes his patron's hopes and fools him into thinking that he may still win Desdemona. Left alone, Iago admits to himself that money and amusement are his real reasons for befriending Roderigo. Then he begins to plan the deception of Othello which will afford him revenge for his many grievances against the Moor.

Commentary

The scene opens with a rather lengthy conference concerning how Venice must deal with its Turkish enemy. Assembled in the Venetian Council Chamber is the governing body of the state, headed by the Duke. All are pondering the conflicting, dangerous news which has been sent to them from Cyprus and from which they find no clear statement as to the size of the Turkish fleet nor its exact destination. None, however, underestimates the very real danger involved; each is sure that the enemy intends to move against the Venetians by attacking Cyprus, despite the fact that a newly arrived sailor reports that one Signior Angelo, who is not identified here nor heard of again, insists that the Turks are headed for Rhodes and not for Cyprus. One senator argues that, in view of the importance of Cyprus, an island which the enemy covets, the apparent move toward Rhodes must be an obvious ruse to catch the Cyprians off guard. The Duke agrees. Then a messenger from Montano, Governor of Cyprus, enters: the fleet approaching Rhodes has joined with a reinforcing fleet; now the entire fleet sails toward Cyprus.

At this point, Brabantio, Othello, Iago, Roderigo, and some officers enter the chamber. The fact that the Duke addresses the Moor immediately, not even noticing Senator Brabantio, is another indication of the extent to which Venice places its hopes on "valiant Othello" (48) – more evidence, that is, of Othello's high status as the hero of the play, the man who has been singled out to conquer "the general enemy Ottoman" (49).

Because Brabantio, an aristocratic senator, is so overwrought, matters of state are shelved momentarily as he makes his startling charges and appeals for help. In fact, his grief is so copious that, at first, the

Duke and the others believe that Desdemona must be dead. Continuing, Brabantio characterizes Desdemona as being the victim of "spells and medicine" (61). Otherwise, how could "nature so prepost'rously . . . err" (62)? Only by using witchcraft could his daughter's heart have been "stol'n" (60) by a black man. The Duke attempts to quiet Brabantio with the assurance that the culprit will be dealt with in accordance with the "bloody book of law" (67). When the aggrieved father points to Othello as the man against whom these charges are brought, the members of the council all react with unanimous consternation.

Othello's defense is the first of many of his major speeches in this play, and there is much to be noted and remembered in this speech, for it helps us to understand why such a noble and stable individual would reject reason and willingly, as it were, become a victim of love's passion and elope with the senator's daughter. With simple dignity, apologizing for his "rudeness" (lack of polish), the Moor addresses his "unvarnish'd tale" (90) to the group, conceding that he indeed has married Brabantio's daughter, but he denies that he did so by means of witchcraft. He presents to the Duke and the others a portrait of himself as a man who has spent almost all of his life in the field as a successful, active soldier. Humbly, he submits he knows nothing of witchcraft and little of the world, for that matter, save that which pertains to warfare.

Brabantio's impassioned speech which follows Othello's quiet statements of fact is ineffectual. It is grounded in racial prejudice and supported only by such shabby phrases as "in spite of nature" (96) and "against all rules of nature" (101). It is clearly Brabantio, not Desdemona, who finds Othello something "fear'd to look on" (98) in contrast to the fair-skinned Venetian men.

Quite reasonably, the Duke points out that Brabantio must substantiate his charges. But Othello, wanting to put an immediate end to this ridiculous accusation, asks that Desdemona herself be brought forth to speak, adding that if he is found to be guilty by her testimony, he will not protest any sentence imposed upon him.

While the Duke awaits Desdemona, Othello delivers his second memorable soliloquy. In it, he reveals that in the past Brabantio himself has shown high regard for Othello; "her father lov'd me," says Othello, and "oft invited me [to his house]" (128), where he urged the Moor to tell him stories of his adventurous, exciting life, filled with "disastrous chances" (134), "moving accidents by flood and field" (135), and "hair-breadth scapes" (136). Here, Othello recalls stories about his being captured and enslaved, about cannibals and about certain "Anthropophagi," men whose heads grew "beneath their shoulders" (145). (Lest one should dwell too long on the matter of these "Anthropophagi," it should be stated that Greek romances, popular in Shakespeare's time, often included accounts of such fabulous barbarians. Othello was not indulging in self-aggrandizement to impress Desdemona or her father.)

The picture we have here of Othello, then, is of a spellbinding raconteur, regaling Brabantio and his daughter with tales of romantic daring. Little wonder that Desdemona would have been enthralled by this exotic man of action and thereby neglect the "wealthy curled darlings" (68) of Venice. Desdemona "lov'd me for the dangers I had pass'd," Othello says. "This only is the witchcraft I have us'd" (167/69).

The Duke's response to Othello's frankness is warmly humorous; he's convinced that "this tale would win my daughter too" (171), and he counsels Brabantio to "take up this mangled matter at the best" (173) – that is, to make the best he can of this situation.

Considering that the play is set approximately in the late sixteenth century, Desdemona's defense of her actions is remarkably forthright, spirited, and courageous. Clearly, she was aware of the great risk involved when she married a man of another race and, moreover, one so completely different from her Venetian suitors. Her ten brief lines are models of concise rationale. Hers, she says, was and is a "divided duty" (181): she remains bound to her noble father for her "life and education" (182); he remains her "lord of duty" (184), and she will always honor him as such. Now, however, she has a husband, and she must recognize her duties to him, just as her mother did to Brabantio.

Brabantio is crushed; he is a defeated man who realizes that the Moor did neither steal nor bewitch his daughter. But he will never understand how his "jewel" (195) renounced all of his paternal guidance and secretly married a man of a different race and nation.

The Duke then informs Othello of the Turks' plan to attack Cyprus and that he, as the leader best informed about the fortifications of the island, must "slubber the gloss of your new fortunes" (228) (delay any shining anticipations of a honeymoon) and turn his full attention upon the enterprise against the Turks – that is, these two lovers, just newly married, are to be separated because of a national crisis. And,

as another example of his high character, Othello promptly acknowledges that public duty takes precedence over private desires.

Then a dramatic element of surprise occurs. When Othello asks
that his wife be properly looked after in his absence, and the Duke
suggests that she stay in her father's household, Brabantio forbids it.
Othello, likewise, forbids it. And Desdemona herself rejects any such
solution. She married the Moor because she did "love . . . to live with
him" (249). Othello himself voices the same sentiments. His is a rational love, he says; thus he suggests that Desdemona come with him.
He asks the council not to think that he will neglect duty "to comply
with [the] heat" (264) of sexual desire or that he will ignore their
"serious and great business scant/ When she is with me" (268-69).
Above all, at no time will he allow her presence to interfere with his
duty to defend Venice against the Turks.

The Duke tells Othello that he can make what arrangements he
likes. The important thing is that he must leave this very night because
"th' affair calls [for] haste" (277). Desdemona is somewhat taken aback
by this order. But notice the Moor's reply: he loves her "with all
[his] heart" (279). Truly, as the Duke notes to Brabantio, Othello "is
far more fair than black" (291). Immediately, there remains only for
the Moor to leave some trusted officer behind, one who will see to
it that Desdemona is brought to Cyprus safely. Tragically, Othello
chooses the very man whom he can trust least in all the world—
"honest Iago" (295).

Brabantio's last words to Othello in this scene are important. As
we shall find, they are packed with irony and provide, in part, an
example of dramatic presaging. "Look to her, Moor" (293), the senator
says. "She has deceiv'd her father, and may thee" (294). (Desdemona
does not deceive Othello, but before long Othello will be so convinced
that she has deceived him that he will murder her.) Othello's reply
to Brabantio is likewise ironic: he vows, "my life upon her faith!" (295).
Shortly, he will take his own life because of his lack of faith in her
faith—in her innocent, chaste fidelity.

The Moor and Desdemona then leave for a last hour together,
and Iago and Roderigo are left alone on the stage. Roderigo is overcome; in marked contrast to the noble, rational lover, Othello, he is
the tormented, rejected lover who can find relief from his misery only
by drowing himself. Iago mocks Roderigo's excessive, posturing
despair over Desdemona's words. Before Iago would drown himself

"for the love of a guinea-hen," he would exchange his "humanity with a baboon" (317-18). To Roderigo's confession that passion controls his will, Iago states that "our bodies are our gardens" and "our wills are gardeners" (323-24). Men, he says, have "reason to cool [their] raging motions" (333). Certainly Iago believes that he himself is a man of controlled will, whose reason is paramount in all his dealings. Hypnotically, he drones commands to Roderigo to "put money in thy purse" (345), all the while assuring him that Desdemona cannot long "continue her love to the Moor" (338). Her love for the Moor had a too "violent commencement" (350); soon she will be "sated with his body" (356), and Moors themselves "are changeable" (352). He so completely dupes his patron, emphasizing that Desdemona will yet be his, that Roderigo agrees to "sell all [his] land" (388).

Throughout his long speech, Iago reveals foremost that he is passion's slave, evidenced by his hatred for Othello, his envy of Othello's power, and his lust for Roderigo's wealth. Cynically, as Roderigo leaves, Iago condemns himself with the well-known line, "Thus do I ever make my fool my purse . . ." (389).

In his last soliloquy in the act, Iago introduces a second motive for his hatred of Othello; he says that it is common gossip that the Moor " 'twixt my sheets . . . [has] done my office" (393-94) and, for Iago, "mere suspicion . . . will do . . . for surety" (395-96). It need hardly be pointed out here that we are listening to a man whose mind is poisoned. There is not the slightest bit of evidence anywhere in this play to indicate that Othello has had an affair with Emilia.

As the act closes, Iago reveals his next malicious plan of action. Aware that Othello trusts him, he will convince the Moor that Cassio is "too familiar" (402) with Desdemona. Othello, he says, "is of a free and open nature" (405); precisely, in Iago's words, Othello is an "ass" — naive, in other words, and we recall that Othello himself has already admitted that he knows "little of this great world . . . [except that which] pertains to feats of broils and battle" (86-87). In the final couplet, which contains the reference to "hell and night" (409) and to "monstrous birth" (410), we sense Iago rubbing his hands in glee; we see all too clearly the unnaturalness and the diabolical elements of his plans to destroy the union of Othello and Desdemona.

ACT II – SCENE 1

Summary

The time advances several weeks, and the curtains open upon the harbor of Cyprus. A fierce storm at sea has crippled the Turkish fleet and has also delayed the course of Othello's voyage. At Cyprus, Governor Montano greets Cassio, whose ship is the first to arrive; shortly afterward, Iago's ship also arrives, with Desdemona on board. To assuage Desdemona's anxiety for Othello's safety, Iago jokes and composes verses, and Cassio also distracts her attention in amiable conversation. Iago privately notes Cassio's behavior toward Desdemona and plans to entrap him later by spreading gossip about him and Desdemona.

Finally Othello arrives; he is joyously reunited with Desdemona and embraces her. When the others have left the stage, Iago convinces Roderigo that Desdemona actually loves Cassio and urges Roderigo to pick a fight with the lieutenant that night. When he is alone, Iago discloses in a soliloquy that he has vague suspicions about both Othello's and Cassio's affairs with Emilia.

Commentary

Now that the major characters have been introduced, and we are aware that a national crisis threatens the city-state of Venice, and that Othello's union with Desdemona is also threatened, the action of the play moves from Venice to the island of Cyprus. Montano, the governor of the island, is anxiously awaiting word of Othello's ship. Othello will replace Montano as governor, but the Moor's ship is somewhere at sea, battling a great storm: "A fuller blast ne'er shook our battlements" (6), Montano says; it is unusually severe and has become a "high-wrought flood" (2), a "wind-shak'd surge" (13), and a "high and monstrous mane" (13). Were it not for its threat to Othello, we realize, this hurricane-like storm would be welcomed because it would probably mean the destruction of the Turkish fleet.

The safe arrival of Cassio is suddenly announced, but before the newly appointed lieutenant makes his actual appearance onstage, Montano and another gentleman again express their concern for the Moor. Again we have public testimony of Othello's unusual superiority as a man and as a martial commander. He will make "a worthy governor" (30), Montano comments, one who will be brave because he "commands/ Like a full soldier" (35-36).

Cassio's entrance is accompanied by more praise for the Moor, and he evidences added concern for Othello and his crew on this "dangerous sea" (46). He finds comfort in the knowledge that Othello's ship is "stoutly timber'd" (48) and that Othello's pilot is an expert. Suspense is the central emotion here. Within moments, Cassio and Montano's men are alerted that a sail has been sighted by the towns-people gathered on the coast. Cassio fervently expresses his hopes that it is Othello's ship, for it is upon Othello that he bases all his hopes. Guns are fired, and Cassio then reveals to Montano the good news of Othello's marriage. Desdemona, he says, is a woman who surpasses "description and wild fame" (62). To Cassio, she is "divine Desdemona" (73) and the "great captain's captain" (74). Cassio then voices a prayer to "Great Jove" (77) that Othello might be well guarded, might presently "bless this bay with his tall ship" (79), and might be reunited with Desdemona. What is significant in this scene is the emphasis on Cassio's utter devotion to his general. While he is certainly in awe of the lovely Desdemona, it is clear that he is an honorable man, one who would not and could not betray the Moor (as Iago will try to prove later). Cassio's character is clearly antithetical to that of Iago, a man who passionately covets the lieutenant's position.

Dramatically, just after we have heard extravagant claims about her, Desdemona enters, accompanied by Iago, Emilia, and several attendants. Cassio's appreciation of his general's lady becomes even more venerated here. He is so overcome that he enjoins all present to bow to her and to hail to her as if she were the Virgin herself, coming with "the grace of heaven,/ Before, behind thee, and on every hand" (85-86). Cassio's effusiveness here can be explained, in part, by the fact that he is a Florentine. This same courtly manner, in fact, encourages him to kiss Emilia moments later.

After a brief word of thanks to Cassio, Desdemona's first words are inquiries after her husband, and it should be pointed out here that throughout the subsequent action leading up to the arrival of Othello, the Moor's well-being remains her foremost concern.

Iago's comments in this scene about his wife, Emilia, are unnecessarily tart, and Desdemona is quick to defend her friend. For the most part, Iago is posturing here; instead of ridiculing the faults of Emilia, he is actually trying to assume a brusque, "manly" pose by deriding his wife. He fools no one. By the nature of the play, we are certain that Emilia cannot be a shrew. She must be young and attractive enough to attract the harmless (and this should be emphasized) gallantry of Cassio, and she must also be attractive enough that Iago can convince himself (if indeed he is capable of truly caring about her) that there may be an excuse for believing that she is unfaithful. Iago's anti-female bombast here adds one of the few touches of comedy in this play but it is often too coarse. Already we are aware that his attitude toward love between men and women is completely cynical.

At this point, Desdemona's discourse with Iago might perhaps seem awkward. Because we have seen so little of Desdemona, and because we witnessed only one example of her spirited nature (when she proclaimed her love for Othello and vowed *not* to be housed in her father's house while Othello was sent to Cyprus), we are not wholly prepared for her to be so witty, nor so sharply able to parry Iago's salty banter. When the two cease their verbal duel, Iago emerges in this scene as a "most profane and liberal [licentious] counsellor" (165), according to Desdemona. Her label is accurate and well-spoken by a woman who, we must remember, is a well-born and well-educated daughter of a Venetian senator. It is conceivable that she has been trained to adapt herself easily to any social situation. She was certainly headstrong in her choice of a husband and equally cool in her defense of him. She will demonstrate this adaptable talent later in the play; it seems to be behavior that is not particularly difficult. She recognizes that Iago is a showoff who prides himself in being impertinent, and thus she never loses her poise nor her overriding concern for her husband. As for Iago, he knows exactly how far he can approach the obscene without offending those present. And, of course, he has the good-mannered Cassio to explain and apologize that his jesting is merely that of a "soldier"—in contrast to Cassio's own background, which we recall has already been damned by Iago as being scholarly, instead of practical and military.

Iago despises this well-mannered Florentine, yet he is abnormally interested in Cassio's Renaissance gallantry—his taking Desdemona by the palm, his "smile upon her" (170), and his kissing her three fingers. He tells us here how he will capitalize on Cassio's good manners: "With as little a web as this [gallant manner] will I ensnare as great a fly as Cassio" (169-70). All this is consistent with what we have seen before. Iago will stop at nothing to ruin the reputation of the man who superseded him and, at the same time, extinguish the love between Othello and Desdemona.

The Moor and his attendants arrive, and the mood of the scene changes as Othello exchanges affectionate greetings with Desdemona, his "fair warrior" (184). Lines 185-95 are the words of a great poet as the Moor speaks of his soul's joy that he has survived the storm at sea and that he is now gazing on his wife. He has triumphed over a terrifying tempest, and he describes it in lines whose cadence conveys the very turbulence of that great storm, with its "hills of seas/ Olympus-high" (189-90). He has suffered "hell" and is now in "heaven" and would be content to die. He has his Desdemona, his "soul's joy" (186). In a sense, he is in a "paradise" of sorts. He has just passed through one kind of hell, one that tried every fiber of his body; shortly, he will pass through another kind of hell, one that will challenge his soul. Othello's happy reunion with Desdemona is accompanied by her prayer that their loves and comforts "increase" and also by Othello's fervent "amen" to that prayer.

Iago's immediate aside lends itself to any actor who yearns to play a master villain. The situation is "well tun'd" (202), he says, but shortly he will see that a different tune will be played in this game of life. He fancies himself to be a sort of musical puppeteer, toying with the emotions and fate of all those around him—with one end: he will destroy the Moor, and soon the beautiful harmonies of natural love will be replaced by the unnatural discords of jealousy and pain.

All this is followed by Othello's next speech, which declares good news: "the Turks are drown'd" (204). Again he stresses the natural harmony of his and Desdemona's love for one another, almost as a counterpoint to Iago's evil words and certainly as an ironic omen of an ideal which is about to be shattered. Here, Othello seems almost too noble, for his exit is accompanied by an order to "good Iago" (209) to go "to the bay and disembark my coffers" (210). Plainly, he believes Iago to be completely trustworthy.

The conversation between Iago and Roderigo, after all the others are gone, is manipulated by Iago so that the gullible Roderigo is given a thorough brainwashing. Iago convinces him that Desdemona is in love with Lieutenant Cassio, and he cites "with what violence she first lov'd the Moor" (225). This infatuation, he says, has been transferred to Cassio; already she finds no delight in looking on the devil—that is, Othello. "Sport" (230) has made her blood "dull" (229), and it desires now to be enflamed. Iago alludes to the Moor as being a man who won her with his "bragging" (225) and "fantastical lies" (226); now she tires of this older man and will soon "heave the gorge, disrelish and abhor the Moor" (235-36). This is some of the most offensive language in the entire play. The imagery, however, with its stress on the physical, the unnatural appetite, and vomiting, is typical of Iago.

Iago then damns Cassio's charms as being those of a "slipper[y] and subtle knave" (245). The lieutenant's eye, he says, can "stamp and counterfeit advantages" (246) and, what's more, he is "handsome, young, and hath all those requisites in him that folly and green minds look after" (250-51). Contemptuously, Iago says that one such "green mind" is Desdemona's and that she "hath found him already" (252).

The simple Roderigo is unbelieving. He has heard Desdemona praised to the heavens; he cannot believe that she – a woman of such "blessed" character – would be attracted to the "knavish" Cassio. Yet Iago prods Roderigo's disbelief by recalling how she did "paddle with the palm of [Cassio's] hand" (259). To Iago, this was leachery, warmly offered from the hand of a "vital" woman – certainly no "blessed" woman, indeed! Such "paddling" of palms, says Iago, is the prologue to the whole "history of lust and foul thoughts" (263). Cassio and Desdemona are animals, he says, and she is no better than any woman – ever on the watch for a handsome man – and, who knows? It might as well be Roderigo, now that she's bored with the Moor.

Iago then explains his plan. Roderigo must find some excuse to anger Cassio; he suggests "speaking too loud" (275) or "discrediting" Cassio – anything that will make Cassio lose control of himself. Cassio's cheerful, courteous demeanor is only veneer, Iago lies; he says that Cassio is "rash and very sudden in choler" (278). If Roderigo can provoke Cassio into fighting, Iago can convince the Cyprians to mutiny when they see what an undisciplined officer commands them. Cassio will then be dismissed, and Desdemona will lose interest in him and be ripe for Roderigo's amorous attentions.

Roderigo takes the bait, and Iago is left alone onstage. In a long soliloquy, he assures himself (and tries to assure us) that Cassio loves Desdemona; "I do well believe 't" (295). This is a measure of how thoroughly he can convince himself of what was earlier an embroidered lie in his web to ensnarl Roderigo. Clearly, Iago believes that Desdemona loves Cassio. And, then, in one of the most surprising statements of the entire play, Iago gives Othello full credit for being such a "constant, loving, noble nature . . . [that] he'll prove to Desdemona/ A most dear husband" (298-300). This stated, he next admits that *he* loves Desdemona, but with a love that has no sexual basis; instead, he loves her as an object which affords him the opportunity to revenge himself on Othello. For the second time, he voices his conviction that the Moor has had a love affair with Emilia, concluding that he will get even — "wife for [wife]" (308). He is confident that he can poison Othello with a jealousy "so strong/ That judgement cannot cure" (310-11). Ending his soliloquy, he confesses that he is not really concerned with Roderigo's fate — "this poor trash of Venice" (312) (Iago even suspects Roderigo of having had an affair with Emilia). His master plan, he sighs, is almost complete; just the details need working out: " 'Tis here, but yet confus'd" (320). Chiefly, it will depend on his corrupting Othello's "peace and quiet/ Even to madness" (319-20).

ACT II – SCENE 2

Summary

Othello's herald proclaims a night of feasting and festivity to celebrate the destruction of the Turkish fleet and also to celebrate the wedding of Othello to Desdemona.

Commentary

This short scene is occasionally combined with the scene that follows. Chiefly, it functions in approximately the same way that a curtain is pulled in a modern theater to indicate the passing of time. We know that the Turkish fleet has suffered "perdition," largely due to the "noble" and "valiant" efforts of Othello, and that the rejoicing celebrates the military victory and also the general's recent marriage. In short, the Moor has proclaimed a holiday to be held from five o'clock until eleven, during which the soldiers and citizens can dance, make bonfires, or make "revels [however] his [addiction] leads him" (6). Dramatically, this mood of merrymaking and celebration is a strong contrast to the tragedy that is about to follow and, in addition, the chaos will give Iago sufficient time and opportunity to set his traps for the unsuspecting Othello. Also, this feasting and dancing will take place at night, and earlier Iago proclaimed that "hell and night/ Must bring this monstrous birth [of his evil design] to the world's light" (I.ii. 409-10). This scene preludes that horror.

ACT II – SCENE 3

Summary

Othello retires for the night with Desdemona, leaving Cassio in charge of the night watch. In a hall of the castle, against the background of the night's merrymaking, Iago succeeds with wine and song in making Cassio drunk and quarrelsome. Urged by Iago to start an altercation, Roderigo follows Cassio offstage; quickly the two men reappear, fighting. Governor Montano interferes in an attempt to stop them and accuses Cassio of being drunk. Enraged, Cassio turns on him and wounds the governor as Roderigo hurries to sound the general alarm. Disturbed by the alarm bell, Othello comes onstage and halts the fighting, demanding to know what caused it. After Iago's seemingly reluctant description of the disturbance, Othello finds Cassio at fault and immediately relieves him of his rank. Iago and Cassio remain behind as the wounded Montano is led off and the others follow. Cassio, sobered, regrets the loss of his military status and reputation, but Iago persuades him that perhaps he can regain Othello's favor again – with Desdemona's "help." After Cassio leaves, Iago gloats over his successful, although seemingly innocent, scheming.

Roderigo returns, sore and full of complaints after his beating. Iago soothes his patron's impatience with platitudes and points out that their success has caused Cassio's discharge. Dawn is coming and it promises good things for them; the two men part as day breaks.

Commentary

Othello, Desdemona, Cassio, and several attendants enter a hall of the castle. The celebration has lasted for several hours, and the Moor instructs "good Michael" (Cassio) to stand guard during the night. His brief speech deserves attention in view of the subsequent change later in both Cassio and Othello. He cautions himself – and also Cassio – not to "outsport discretion" (3) – that is, they should not allow the partying to get out of hand nor last too long. He, for example, has acknowledged but has not shared in the abundant toasts, for he must not neglect his duties. His men and this island must be supervised, above all. Speaking to Desdemona, he says that only now does he look forward to some peaceful intimacy "to come 'tween me and you" (10). He counsels prudence for all, and Cassio answers that Iago has given "direction" (4). To this, Othello answers that he is satisfied: "Iago is most honest" (6).

When Iago enters, we hear that the reveling has lasted not quite five hours. Insinuatingly, he remarks that Othello left watch duty early to "wanton the night" (16) with Desdemona. But to all of Iago's carnal remarks, Cassio is deaf. To Cassio, Desdemona is "most exquisite" (18), "fresh and delicate" (20), "modest" (26), and "indeed perfection" (28). Iago scoffs at Cassio's platonic platitudes ("Well, happiness to their sheets!" (29)) and invites Cassio to have "a stoup of wine" (30). But not even Cassio's courteous excuses can stop Iago's determination. Iago *insists* on the two men sharing a drink; their friendship and the nature of the occasion demand it. Repeatedly, Cassio refuses. He's already had a drink – and even that drink he diluted; very simply, he feels that he shouldn't drink any more. He already feels the "innovation" (40) of that one drink, and he "dare not task my weakness with any more" (45). Iago then tries to detain him by asking him, at least, to call in some of the other men for a drink or two. Alone, Iago reveals his next schemings: already he has seen to it that Roderigo and the guardsmen have imbibed freely – "carous'd/ Potations pottle-deep" (55-56), he calls it, meaning that they've tipped the bottoms of their tankards in toasts most of the night. "Now," he says, " 'mongst this flock of drunkards/ Am I to put our Cassio in some action/ That may offend the isle" (61-63).

The drinking episode that follows is a lively one. Governor Montano joins the group, and Iago sets the tone with his drinking song, playing to perfection the role of the hail-fellow-well-met. Cassio does indeed become drunk, his tongue becomes thick, and his movements wavering. Yet he insists that he is *not* drunk – and all the others agree with him as he staggers from the stage.

Iago's plan is proceeding with perfection; his depravity is shocking. He calculated carefully on the mannerly Florentine's over-indulging simply because good manners called for him to celebrate the victory and to pacify the pleadings of Othello's ensign; it was out of courtesy that he began drinking, despite his self-admitted weakness. And note that almost immediately after Cassio leaves, Iago begins to complain excessively about the young lieutenant's "vice," making it seem that Cassio would be a model soldier, were it not for his vice of alcoholism, which is sadly condoned by Othello. This is a blatant lie. Then with equal oiliness, Iago expresses concern and anxiety about the fate of Cyprus, sighing that he does "love Cassio well; and would do much/ To cure him of this evil [drinking]" (148-49).

The next episode of this scene focuses on the drunken Cassio in pursuit of the hapless Roderigo, whom he denounces as a rogue and as a rascal. The governor endeavors to intercede, and Cassio turns on him, giving Iago the chance to instruct Roderigo what to do. The "dupe" is told to raise a general alarm while Iago assumes the role of "peacemaker." Othello, accompanied by armed men, arrives to find that the governor has been wounded by Cassio. Iago's plans have succeeded far beyond any of his expectations.

Another opportunity for tour-de-force acting occurs when Othello makes inquiries about the reason for "this barbarous brawl" (172), and Iago must answer. The villainous ensign holds back, seemingly, appearing to be reluctant to inform against a friend. Nor can the drunken lieutenant nor the wounded governor provide many of the details. The Moor is appalled to find that such a "private and domestic quarrel" (215) should take place when the safety of Cyprus should be the concern of all. Iago answers, hypocritically, that he would rather have his tongue cut out than "do offense to Cassio" (222). He then prattles sufficiently until Othello determines that Cassio must be punished. In fact, he believes that Iago's words against Cassio are probably too soft and that he "doth mince this matter" (247). Therefore, despite the fact that Othello loves Cassio well, he strips him of his rank.

After everybody but Iago and Cassio have exited, the ex-lieutenant mourns the reputation which he has lost, and he curses the power of alcohol: "To be now a sensible man, by and by a fool, and presently a beast!" (309-10). Iago is ready with facile words of consolation. He assures Cassio that he has only to wait until the Moor is in a better mood. And, better yet, he reminds Cassio, the Moor is not *really* a general – that position, in truth, belongs to Desdemona, for Othello "hath devoted and given up himself" (321-22) to her. Both Othello and Desdemona are such simple people, Iago implies sarcastically; moreover, he is quite sure that Desdemona deems it a "vice in her goodness not to do more than she is requested" (326-27). Therefore, Cassio should speak to her. Cassio understands instantly:

if he asks her to intercede with the Moor, all will be set to rights again. Naively, Cassio concedes that Iago does "advise me well" (332), to which Iago protests "in the sincerity of love and honest kindness" (334). Shakespeare's layering of villainy upon Iago becomes, at times, almost too heavy, but occasionally, as here, it is briefly lightened by Iago's amoral wit, as evidenced here, when Iago assesses the situation.

Alone, Iago asks how it is possible that anyone could term him a villain. Surely Desdemona's generous nature will try to heal the breach between Cassio and her husband; Iago strives for no more than what would seem true and possible. Yet he interrupts his soliloquy with a cynical cry: "Divinity of hell!" (356). In effect, he is celebrating his god: evil itself, colored in all its corruptions with ironical words of purity. Using Desdemona and her natural goodness, Iago will "turn her virtue into pitch,/ And . . . make the net/ That shall enmesh them all" (366-68).

As the act ends, Roderigo, the simple gull, reenters and complains of having little money left and that he has been "well cudgell'd" (372). He's ready to go back to Venice, but Iago's thoughts are ever on Roderigo's bountiful pocketbook, and so he promises him that morning will bring better things. Alone again, he reveals two more of his machinations: Emilia must ask Desdemona to speak to the Moor about Cassio, and Iago will try to position the Moor so that he sees his wife and the young, courtly ex-lieutenant in close conversation.

ACT III – SCENE 1

Summary

Cassio brings in some musicians to "serenade" the newly wedded couple, and Othello's clown, or jester, comes in to entertain the group. This done, the musicians are paid and they exit. At this point, Iago arrives and helps Cassio arrange a private meeting with Desdemona. After Iago leaves, Emilia enters and, at Cassio's request, takes him to talk with Desdemona.

Commentary

This scene serves as a kind of comic relief – that is, it gives the audience's emotions a brief pause from the tension of the preceding acts and offers the audience some respite before it is plunged into the highly emotional scenes that follow very swiftly. The setting is next morning, outside the castle, where Cassio has arranged for a group of musicians to entertain Othello and Desdemona. In addition to the musicians, there is a clown, or jester, a figure that appears in many Renaissance plays and could be counted on to entertain the audience with his physical nimbleness and his witty double entendres. Here the clown makes humorous reference to "wind" instruments and purposely confuses "tails" and "tales" in several coarse puns before he pokes fun at the musicians' performance. Othello does not care for the music, and so the clown dismisses them with money and bids them to "vanish into the air, away!" (21).

Cassio then gives the clown a gold piece and instructs him to tell Emilia, "the gentlewoman that attends the [General's wife]" (26-27), that he (Cassio) wishes to talk with her.

Iago enters as the clown exits and notes that Cassio has not been to bed yet. Cassio confirms it; he has decided to follow Iago's suggestion and talk with Emilia and see if she can convince Desdemona to speak with him. Iago is obviously pleased and offers to keep the Moor busy so that the "converse and business" (40) of Cassio and Desdemona "may be more free" (41). The dramatic irony here is that Iago hopes to keep Othello "busy" while Cassio and Desdemona are talking together, meaning that the Moor will be "busy" observing his wife and his courtly ex-lieutenant exchanging serious conversation. Upon Iago's exit, Cassio remarks that he "never knew/ A Florentine more kind and honest" (42-43). The irony here is self-evident. Hopefully, *many* Florentines are more honest than Iago and, hopefully, most Florentines are not as naive as young Cassio.

Emilia enters and greets the Moor's ex-lieutenant and expresses her disappointment and sorrow at his misfortunes. From her, Cassio happily learns that already Desdemona "speaks . . . stoutly" (47) to her husband in Cassio's defense, but because Cassio wounded Cyprus's governor, a man of "great fame . . . and great affinity" (48-49), Othello cannot yet reinstate Cassio as his lieutenant. Yet, Desdemona thinks that there may be some hope, for Othello "protests he loves you,/ And . . . [will] take the safest [soonest] occasion . . . to bring you in again" (50-53). The news is indeed good and should satisfy Cassio, but fate makes Cassio too impatient to resume his lieutenancy. Thus he beseeches Emilia to arrange for him to speak with Desdemona alone. Emilia agrees.

ACT III – SCENE 2

Summary

Othello gives some letters to Iago to be posted and tells him that he will be walking around the grounds of the castle with some gentlemen and requests that Iago meet him later.

Commentary

Othello instructs Iago to see to it that certain letters are sent *immediately* to the Venetian Senate and then rejoin him. He then leaves to inspect the Cyprian fortifications. This scene is extremely brief, consisting of less than ten lines, but it functions to show that Othello is very busy and that he is engaged in business of the state. Iago, therefore, realizes that the time is opportune for him to act: Desdemona is free and if Iago can make the necessary arrangements, he can bring Cassio and Desdemona together so that Cassio can plead his case; moreover, the possibility exists that Iago can even arrange to have Othello secretly witness a meeting between his wife and his ex-lieutenant.

ACT III – SCENE 3

Summary

In the castle garden, Desdemona promises Cassio that she will do all that she can to persuade Othello to reinstate the ex-lieutenant. As Othello and Iago enter, Cassio leaves hurriedly. As Othello is approaching his wife, Iago quickly takes the opportunity to draw Othello's attention to Cassio's "guilty" leave-taking. Desdemona launches at once into a petition for Cassio, continuing good-humoredly, yet insistently, until Othello grants her plea.

As Desdemona and Emilia withdraw, Iago begins sinister and bitter insinuations about Cassio, forcing Othello to recall that Cassio was often instrumental in Othello's courtship of Desdemona. Considering deeply what he hears, Iago pretends to be astonished. He "ponders" and Othello asks him to make plain what he is thinking, but Iago adroitly evades answering until he has fully aroused Othello's curiosity. Then he cunningly warns Othello against jealousy, the "green-ey'd monster" (166). Othello answers confidently that he will harbor no suspicions unless they can be proved. Iago then boldly suggests a hypothetical affair between Cassio and Desdemona and, in several ways, he begins to undermine Othello's faith in Desdemona's innocence. After Iago has left, Othello is somewhat reassured when Desdemona returns. She tries to soothe his aching head with her handkerchief, but he says irritably that it is too small and pushes it from him; it falls to the floor unnoticed. As they depart, it is left behind.

Emilia picks up the strawberry-embroidered handkerchief, Othello's first intimate gift to Desdemona, gives it to Iago, and exits. Othello reenters then, his mind fermenting with the doubts planted by Iago. He demands proof, immediate and positive, that his wife is guilty of infidelity. Iago claims that while spending a night with Cassio he himself overheard Cassio talking in a dream about making love to Desdemona. He also says that he has seen Cassio wipe his beard with a handkerchief embroidered in a strawberry pattern. Enraged, Othello sinks to his knees. He is joined by Iago, and together they vow sacred revenge. On rising, Othello announces that Iago will be his new lieutenant.

Commentary

This scene, often called the "temptation scene," is the most important scene in the entire play and one of the most well-known scenes in all drama. In it, Iago speaks carefully and at length with Othello and plants the seeds of suspicion and jealousy which eventually bring about the tragic events of the play. Ironically, it is Desdemona's innocent attempt to reconcile Othello with Cassio that gives Iago the opportunity to wreak vengeance upon Othello, thereby causing the murder and suicide which bring this tragedy to its violent conclusion.

Ironically also, when the curtains for this act part, they reveal the loveliest scene in the entire play: the garden of the Cyprian castle. Desdemona, the well-meaning bride, has been talking with Cassio and tells him that she is sure that she can influence her husband in Cassio's behalf.

Emilia is present and adds her own good wishes for Cassio; she too hopes that Desdemona will be successful. But when Emilia adds that her husband, Iago, grieves "as if the cause were his" (4) that Cassio has lost his position and that his friendship with the Moor has been severed, even the most casual listener in the audience would probably gasp in disbelief. This is followed by an equally startling comment:

Desdemona, speaking of Iago, says, "O, that's an honest fellow" (5). The dramatic irony is especially keen here as Desdemona tells Cassio that she is convinced that she "will have [her] lord and [him] again/ As friendly as [they] were" (6-7).

Cassio expresses his gratitude, but he urges Desdemona not to delay, for if Othello waits too long to appoint a new lieutenant, he may "forget my love and service" (18). Again, Desdemona is most reassuring, stating that it is not in her character to violate a vow of friendship. (Later, Othello will believe not only that she has violated a vow of friendship, but that she has violated their vows of marriage.) Comically, Desdemona jests to Cassio that she will "talk him [Othello] out of patience;/ His bed shall seem a school . . . I'll intermingle everything he does/ With Cassio's suit" (23-26). (This too is ironically ominous; within an hour, Othello's notion of his marriage bed will be filled with false visions of Cassio.) Desdemona's final lines here are prophetic: as Cassio's solicitor, she would "rather die/ Than give [his] cause away" (27-28).

Emilia then notes that Othello and Iago are approaching. When the Moor and Iago enter, Cassio excuses himself hurriedly, saying that he is too ill at ease to speak with the general at this time. And it is at this point that Iago, a brilliant tactician who is ready to make the most of every incident and occasion, begins to taint Othello's belief in Desdemona's fidelity. Yet he is careful to represent himself as an honest, but reluctant witness. His "Ha! I like not that!" (35) is a blatant lie; this fraudulent tsk-tsking hides Iago's true delight; nothing could satisfy his perversity more. But because Othello sees nothing amiss, Iago must make a show of not wanting to speak of it, or of Cassio, while all the time insinuating that Cassio was not just leaving, but that he was "steal[ing] away so guilty-like" (39). Iago's words here are filled with forceful innuendo, and as he pretends to be a man who cannot believe what he sees, he reintroduces jealousy into Othello's subconscious.

Desdemona greets her husband and, without guilt, introduces Cassio's name into their conversation. Here, fate plays a major role in this tragedy; not even Iago wholly arranged this swift, coinciden-tal confrontation of Othello, Desdemona, and Cassio, and certainly the pathos of Desdemona's position here is largely due to no other factor than fate. And Desdemona could not purposely have chosen a worse time to mention Cassio's name to her husband. In addition, she innocently refers to Cassio as a "suitor." All these coincidences will fester later in Othello's subconscious as Iago continues to fire the Moor's jealousy. But for now, Othello is without suspicion, even as his wife speaks openly of Cassio's wish to be reinstated as his lieutenant and of her own wish for their reconciliation. She sees no villainy in Cassio's face, she says; Cassio "errs in ignorance and not in cunning" (49). As another example of dramatic irony, note how clearly we see the contrast between Cassio and Iago, a man who certainly errs—at least morally—in his own "cunning."

But Othello seems to be concerned with other matters. Obviously, he will do what his wife asks, but his thoughts are on other things. He does not wish to call Cassio back at the moment, but Desdemona is insistent. Perhaps she is merely young and eager to have her requests granted, or perhaps she is too eager to prove to herself that her new husband is obedient; whatever the reason, she does seem to nag Othello about *when* he will reinstate Cassio as his lieutenant: ". . . to-night at supper? . . . / To-morrow dinner then? . . . / to-morrow night; on Tuesday morn;/ On Tuesday noon, or night; on Wednesday morn./ I prithee, name the time, but let it not/ Exceed three days. . . . When shall he come?/ Tell me, Othello" (57-68). Even though she did promise Cassio not to delay speaking to Othello about the matter, such annoying insistence seems unnecessary, and it leads to Othello's becoming mildly vexed with his wife's childish pestering: "Prithee, no more; let him come when he will,/ I will deny thee nothing" (74-75).

Desdemona realizes that Othello's answer is curt, and she emphasizes that this is an important matter and not a trifle that she is asking. To this, Othello stresses again that he will deny her nothing but, in return, he asks for a bit of time so that he can be alone; he will join her shortly.

As Desdemona leaves, Othello chides himself for being irritated by his wife. Lovingly he sighs, "Excellent wretch! Perdition catch my soul,/ But I do love thee! and when I love thee not,/ Chaos is come again" (90-92). There is an element of prophecy here not only in Desdemona's and Othello's farewells to one another, but also in their lines and in the remainder of the Moor's first speech after Desdemona leaves. In a metaphorical sense, perdition will soon catch Othello's soul, and chaos will soon replace order in his life.

When Iago is alone with Othello, he resumes his attack on his general's soul. Out of seemingly idle curiosity, he asks if Desdemona

was correct when she referred to the days when Othello was court-
ing her; did Cassio indeed "know of your love?" (95). Here he prods
Othello's memory to recall that Desdemona and Cassio have known
each other for some time. Then again playing the reluctant confidant,
he begs, as it were, not to be pressed about certain of his dark
thoughts. One can see how skillfully he makes use of his public reputation for honesty, and it is necessary to remind oneself throughout the
play and especially in this scene that Iago does have a reputation for
complete honesty. It is for this reason that Othello is alarmed by Iago's
hesitations and "pursed brow"; Othello knows that Iago is not a "false
disloyal knave" (121) and that he is "full of love and honesty" (118).
If Iago fears something, it must be a concern "working from the heart"
(123). Othello is convinced that Iago is withholding something and
asks for his ruminations, the "worst of thoughts/ The worst of words"
(132-33). What Iago is doing, of course, is making Othello believe that
Iago's honor is at stake if he confesses his fears. Thus he lies to Othello
again, saying that he is unwilling to speak further because he may
be "vicious in [his] guess" (145).

But one should never doubt that Iago *will* speak the "worst of
thoughts" (132), although at first he does not answer directly. First,
he speaks only the word "jealousy" aloud, fixing it in Othello's
imagination; then, sanctimoniously, he warns his general against this
evil, this "green-ey'd monster" (166) and refers to the "wisdom" of
Othello, implying that the general is not one to be trapped by his emotions. Filled with what appears to be moral fervor, Iago then proceeds
to a glorification of *reputation*. One might profitably recall Iago's antithetical views on the same subject when he was talking with Cassio
earlier. In Act II, Scene 3, Iago told Cassio that "reputation is an idle
and most false imposition; oft got without merit, and lost without
deserving" (268-70). Here, Iago seemingly holds reputation in the
highest esteem; it is the "jewel of [a man's] soul" ("who steals my purse
steals trash . . . / But he that filches from me my good name/ Robs
me of that which not enriches him,/ And makes me poor indeed")
(156-61).

Othello hears, and his "O misery!" (171) tells us that already he
has begun to suffer aching pangs of jealousy, even though he has
vowed not to be of a jealous nature. He swears that he will "see before
I doubt; when I doubt, prove" (190). And Iago approves of such a
stance; he, of course, is in a position to let human nature run its course

and "prove" what it wishes—irrationally. He knows that man, being human, is flawed and subject to fears and irrational suspicions. He then asks the Moor to use his "free and noble nature" (199) to determine for himself the truth of the behavior between Desdemona and Cassio. But he reminds Othello that Desdemona is a Venetian lady and "in Venice they [wives] do not let [even God] see the pranks/ They dare not show their husbands" (202-3). In other words, the faithless wife is a well-known member of Venetian society. Here we should recall Othello's words to the Duke of Venice; he confessed that he knew very little of the world except for that pertaining to warfare. Othello is a master of games on the battlefield, but he is innocent of social games. Iago also urges Othello to recall that Desdemona deceived her own father by marrying Othello. To Brabantio, Desdemona pretended to be afraid of Othello's dark looks; she pretended to shake and tremble at Othello's exotic demeanor, yet "she lov'd them [Othello's features] most" (207). The implication is clear; Iago does not have to state it: if Desdemona deceived her own flesh and blood, she might just as naturally deceive her husband.

The logic of these lines is forceful, and Iago is astute enough to pause now and then, begging his superior's forgiveness, and, at the same time, attributing his own frankness to his devotion and regard for Othello. When we hear the Moor say, "I am bound to thee for ever" (213), we feel that indeed he has been irrevocably trapped.

Before the two men part, Iago goes to further pains to make Othello believe in his honesty and also to insure that Othello's jealousy has been sufficiently inflamed. He must also measure how well he has succeeded thus far. Iago stresses that Cassio is his "worthy friend"; in other words, one does not lie about one's friends and, therefore, the Moor must not exaggerate in his imagination what he hears. Yet Iago is certain that Othello has already exaggerated to himself everything he has just heard. For that reason, Iago's remark to Othello that all this has "a little dash'd your spirits" (214) is a gross understatement. Othello is no longer as sure as he was of Desdemona's fidelity, for he ponders on the possibility of ". . . nature erring from itself—" (227). This thought is similar to his father-in-law's observation in Act I, Scene 2, when Brabantio spoke of "nature erring"—when Desdemona "unnaturally" chose Othello, a man not of her own race or color. Othello turns and asks that Iago's wife, Emilia, watch Desdemona closely. Then he bids Iago farewell, painfully asking himself why he married at all; it is obvious to him that "this honest creature [Iago] doubtless/ Sees and knows more, much more, than he unfolds" (242-43).

Now we hear Othello in a soliloquy (258-77), and the range of the imagery which he uses underscores the appalling change in his character. There is only one thing now of which Othello is certain – the "exceeding honesty" of Iago. The Moor is obsessed with the need to prove or disprove Desdemona's fidelity. If he indeed finds her false, he'll "whistle her off and let her down the wind/ To prey at fortune" (262-63) – that is, he will turn her out and make her shift for herself. And here he begins to look for reasons for her unfaithfulness. Convulsed with introspection, he curses his black skin and his lack of social graces and also the fact that he is "into the vale of years" (266) (he is much older than Desdemona) – all these things, he fears, could turn a woman from her husband's bed. This mental agony approaches the emotional climax of the play; here is the first turning point of the drama. Othello's mind and soul are torn with irrational images of Desdemona's infidelity and of his own unworthiness. Othello sees himself as an old man, an old cuckold, one who has treasured Desdemona blindly, beyond reason. Hours ago, he was filled with the spirit of a young bridegroom; now he is reduced to ignominy. Once he felt he was one of the "great ones" (273); now his pride in himself and in Desdemona's love for him is destroyed. Othello is ravaged by self-loathing, reduced to comparing himself to a dungeoned toad; he is cursed by a "destiny unshunnable" (275).

And yet, as Desdemona and Emilia enter, he is able to move from this state of abject hopelessness to a momentary appeal to heaven (278) when he declares that he will *not* believe that his wife is false to him. In his few words with Desdemona, he speaks faintly, pleading that he has a headache. When Desdemona offers to bind his aching head with her handkerchief, he declines because the handkerchief is too small. He pushes it from him and it falls "unnoticed" to the floor. This dropped, unnoticed handkerchief should not escape our notice. Desdemona carries it because she treasures it deeply. It was one of her first gifts from Othello, and he has asked her to keep it with her always, and she has; in fact, Emilia has seen Desdemona, on occasion, kiss the handkerchief and talk to it. Later, this handkerchief in Cassio's possession will be sufficient "proof" for Othello to abandon all faith in Desdemona.

Alone, Emilia picks up the handkerchief. She knows how deeply Desdemona treasures it, but she recalls that Iago has asked her many times to "steal" it. She is puzzled by his request, but now she has an opportunity to have the embroidery pattern copied, and she can give it to her whimsical husband. Here it is significant that twice Emilia uses the verb *steal* and also the verb *filch* when she refers to Iago's request (ll. 293, 309, and 315).

Iago enters and, after a brief exchange with his wife, learns that she has the very handkerchief that he has longed for. He snatches it from her and refuses to tell her why he wants it. After Emilia leaves, he reveals the next step in his plan: he will go to Cassio's lodgings, leave the handkerchief there, and let Cassio find it. Cassio will keep it and then Othello will see it in the ex-lieutenant's possession. By this time, Othello's suspicions will be ripe with Iago's "poison" (325), for "trifles light as air/ Are to the jealous confirmations strong/ As proofs of holy writ" (322-24). Othello will then conclude that Desdemona either gave the handkerchief to Cassio as a token of their love or left it at Cassio's lodgings after a rendezvous. In fact, a conclusion is hardly necessary; for a mind as inflamed with jealousy as Othello's, the handkerchief itself is metaphor enough. Even now Othello's blood "burn[s] like the mines of sulphur" (329). This suggestion of hellfire by Iago is a reflection of his own diabolical role in this villainy.

When Othello enters, it is evident to Iago, and to us, that he is a fallen man. Never more shall he find repose. Neither the opium of poppies nor the distillation of the mandrake root will help him find sleep. Momentarily, Othello seems to revive his senses, snarling at Iago's villainy and sending him away, then he slumps into despair. Iago's evil has "set [the Moor] on the rack" (335), and Othello wishes in vain that he had remained blind to his wife's *alleged* infidelity. In his imagination, he has seen "her stol'n hours of lust . . . [and tasted] Cassio's kisses on her lips" (338-41). He would have been happier, he cries, if his entire company of soldiers had "tasted her sweet body" (346), and he had remained ignorant of the entire episode. But now this mental torment of suspicion gnaws at him until he knows no peace.

The superb "farewell speech" that follows emphasizes how much Othello has lost—he, the model commander, the premier soldier—his "occupation's gone!" (357). Iago appears incredulous, and it is then that Othello turns on him with words that make Iago only too aware of the danger which faces him. At last Othello utters a true appraisal of Iago: "Villain, be sure thou prove my love a whore" (359). But schemer that Iago is, he knows what must be done to protect himself; he must feign another vow of honesty and concern for Othello's welfare. The Moor, he says, has taught him a valuable lesson. "I'll love no friend, sith love breeds such offence" (380). Othello promptly concedes that Iago *is* honest, and the villain knows that for the time being he is safe. He turns to his general and fawns over his master's distress, noting that Othello is "eaten up with passion" (391). Then, in unusually coarse imagery, he introduces the subject of what kind of evidence would resolve Othello's doubts. The bestial images which Iago conjures up reek of base sexuality, for now Iago no longer needs to rely on innuendo. Now he tells Othello a bold lie, claiming that he himself slept beside Cassio recently; kept awake by a raging toothache that night, Iago says that Cassio moaned in his sleep for "Sweet Desdemona" (419) and cautioned her to hide their love. Then Cassio seized Iago's hand, kissed him hard on the mouth, and threw his leg over Iago's thigh, kissing him all the while, and cursing fate, which "gave [Desdemona] to the Moor!" (421-26). This is Iago's "proof" that makes it perfectly clear to him that Cassio has had illicit relations with Desdemona.

Othello is beside himself. "O monstrous! monstrous!" (427) he cries. But again the ingenious Iago is quick to remind his master that, in reality, this was no more than Cassio's *dream*. Othello, however, thinks otherwise – as Iago was certain he would. In his rage, the Moor declares that he will tear Desdemona to pieces. Here, compare this madman, incensed by Iago's poison, with the noble Moor who, only a few hours ago, repeatedly demonstrated such complete command of himself.

Yet Iago must be sure that Othello is sufficiently mad; therefore, he makes reference to Desdemona's handkerchief with its intricate strawberry embroidery; Othello immediately remembers it as the very one he gave to his wife. Iago tells the Moor that only today he saw Cassio "wipe his beard" (439) with it. Othello is enraged to the point where he is convinced that absolutely all of his suspicions are true. "All my fond love thus do I blow to heaven./ 'Tis gone," he exclaims (445-46), and in highly rhetorical lines, he dwells upon "black vengeance" and "tyrannous hate" (446-49).

Iago urges Othello to be patient, arguing that he may change his mind, and there follows the well-known Pontic sea simile, in which Othello compares his "bloody thoughts" (447) to the sea's compulsive current, one which never ebbs but keeps on its course until it reaches its destination, the junction of the Propontic and the Hellespont (453-60). In this simile, Othello stresses his high status (as we might expect a tragic hero to do), identifying himself with large and mighty elements of nature. Equally important, this simile makes clear the absoluteness in Othello's character; once he has decided which course to take, he cannot turn back, and this decision does much to make plausible the almost incredible actions which follow.

Othello solemnly vows to execute "a capable and wide revenge" (459), and then he kneels. He uses such words as *heaven, reverence,* and *sacred,* and it is as though he sees himself as a rightful scourge of evil, as executing *public* justice and not merely doing *personal* revenge. Iago bids the Moor not to rise yet, and he himself kneels and dedicates himself to "wrong'd Othello's service" (467). Then as both rise, Othello "greets" Iago's love and delegates a test of Iago's loyalty: see to it that Cassio is dead within three days. One cannot imagine more welcome words to Iago. As for Desdemona's fate, Othello says that he will withdraw and find "some swift means of death" (447). Othello's soul is so hopelessly ensnared in Iago's web of treachery that he proclaims Iago as his new lieutenant and states tragically, "I am your own for ever" (449).

ACT III – SCENE 4

Summary

Outside the castle, Desdemona sends Othello's clown to bring Cassio to her. When Othello enters, she again pleads with him to reinstate Cassio as his lieutenant, but Othello's only concern is with the lost handkerchief. Desdemona tries to console him, saying that she is certain that it is not lost. Othello warns her that the handkerchief possesses magical powers and that its loss would be a misfortune. Angrily, he leaves when she cannot produce it. Iago and Cassio enter; they too are at a loss to explain Othello's moodiness. When the others have gone, Cassio meets Bianca, his current mistress, who chides him for neglecting her for a week. Cassio changes the subject and gives her a handkerchief that he found in his room, asking her to make a copy of the embroidery. Bianca is disturbed at his neglecting her, but she nevertheless agrees to do what he asks.

Commentary

As a sort of prelude to this scene, we have a brief exchange between Desdemona and Othello's clown. These twenty or so lines of broad comedy tend to relieve the great tension of the last scene and provide a short respite before Desdemona and Othello confront one another again. Yet the comedy here is not particularly amusing; it is too brief and its humor depends on wordplay involving the verb *lie,* the key verb which Iago and Othello will discuss in Act IV, Scene 1, when Iago tells his general that not only did Cassio *lie* with Desdemona, but that he boasted of it.

Outside the castle, Desdemona is anxious to find Cassio; she promised him that she would speak to her husband about reinstating his former lieutenant, and she would like to reassure him that she has spoken to Othello and that he has promised to reappoint Cassio. Desdemona is pleased that Othello will soon be reconciled with Cassio. Ironically, Othello has never felt more hatred for Cassio. Initially, Cassio's accidental stabbing of Montano displeased him, but this was a mere trifle compared to how he now feels about Cassio's (imagined) sexual conquest of Desdemona. Remember, also, that Othello has just pronounced a death sentence on Cassio.

When the clown leaves, Desdemona asks Emilia about the strawberry-embroidered handkerchief. Emilia answers with an outright lie: "I know not, madam" (24). She knows precisely what happened to it; she gave the handkerchief to Iago, but she says nothing. Nor does she correct herself when Desdemona, a few minutes later, tells her how much she values the handkerchief. Nor does Emilia comment when, in a touch of irony, Desdemona says that she would "rather have lost my purse" (25). It is an ironic coincidence that Desdemona would use this particular analogy, for we have just heard Iago tell Othello, in regard to one's reputation (III.iii.156-61), that someone who would steal another's purse "steals trash." This is Desdemona's point precisely, and yet not even she knows how tragically this lost handkerchief will figure in the loss of her reputation. She finds comfort, however, in her belief that her husband is "noble" (26) and "true of mind" (27) and has not the "baseness" (27) of "jealous creatures" (28). Emilia does not have her friend's faith in Othello and asks further about his qualities. Desdemona answers and elaborates on one of many images in this play that characterizes Othello's clear-mindedness. She says that "the sun . . . / Drew all such humours [dark moods] from him" (30-31). These moods, or humours, are absent from his character. Othello may be dark of skin, but he has a strong reputation for being "clear-minded," calm, self-controlled and, most important, for not being a suspicious man.

Desdemona's words are dramatically ironic, for they prepare us for Othello's entrance and for his reaction to his wife. He comes onstage and tries to appear normal, yet we realize immediately that he is drunk with jealousy. He speaks in conundrums, taking Desdemona's hand and commenting on its moistness, then breaking into grave, exaggerated bombast about his wife's hand being "hot, hot, and moist" (39); her hand requires "a sequester from liberty" (40), he says, then sarcastically he praises it as a "good hand,/ A frank one" (43-44). He is suggesting that Desdemona is unchaste; her palm openly indicates that she has strong, sexual desires. She is "liberal" (38) – that is, she gives herself too freely to others. It is as if Iago – and not Othello – were speaking, and the irony here lies in Othello's having too "liberally" (too easily) given his soul to Iago; Othello has been too easily seduced by Iago. Understandably, Desdemona is puzzled by her husband's words: "I cannot speak of this" (48), she says, and changes the subject, reminding Othello of his promise to deny her nothing. She tells him that, at her bidding, Cassio is coming to speak with him. How unfortunately bad her timing is hardly needs to be pointed out. The Moor, however, is not to put aside. He complains of a cold and asks for a handkerchief to see if, in fact, Desdemona can produce the one he asked her to always carry with her. When she hands him one that is not the handkerchief he has in mind, he reproves her: "That's a fault" (55).

It is then that he tells her a fantastic story about an Egyptian gypsy giving a certain handkerchief to his mother; it is a magical handkerchief and carries the power of love, but it also carries a curse. If it is ever lost or given away, disaster will damn its owner. Othello swears the legend is true, that a sibyl herself embroidered it with silk that was spun from sacred worms and dyed with a precious liquid. This, of course, alarms the young and innocent Desdemona; remember that part of Othello's charm was his dark, Moorish looks. Here is dark, exotic lore that threatens to destroy her – all because she has misplaced the treasured heirloom that Othello entrusted to her. We can under-stand her anguished cry to God that she wishes she had "never seen't!" (77). The handkerchief, then, is no mere piece of cloth. It is a part of Othello's past. The handkerchief was important to his mother; she could almost read minds with it; it helped her "subdue" (59) her hus-band's love. It is a symbol of his parents' love, and Othello believes that it is a symbol of the purity of Desdemona's love for him. It is, therefore, no mere prop in Shakespeare's construction of this tragedy. The handkerchief is a sacred talisman, but Desdemona was ignorant of its history and of its significance to her husband.

When Othello hears his wife's outcry, he pounces on her despair and almost overwhelms her with questions, while she naively tries to stop him with pleas that he must see Cassio or, at least, talk to her about Cassio. Repeatedly, he asks for the handkerchief and repeatedly she asks him to think of Cassio. Othello's rage builds and when he can bear no more, he exits.

One wonders what went on in Emilia's mind as she witnessed Othello's fury. She knows that she found the handkerchief and gave it to Iago. She could silence Othello's mad questioning, but she re-mains silent and, after Othello's headstrong exit, she asks if Des-demona believes that Othello is still the noble, clear-minded husband that she just spoke of. Desdemona is ready to acknowledge the hand-kerchief's magic. About her husband's display of temper, she can only answer, "I ne'er saw this before" (100). Emilia's answer to her friend reveals a cynicism that has come from years of living with Iago. She believes that no woman can be certain of her husband; to her, all men are egocentric – "They are all but stomachs, and we all but food;/ They eat us hungerly, and when they are full/ They belch us" (104-6). It is also quite possible that she is jealous of her friend's praise for her "perfect" husband and tired of hearing about Othello's sterling perfec-tion. To her, a handkerchief is nothing more than a handkerchief, and the fact that Othello can berate Desdemona for losing such a trifle is only proof that he is no different than any other man.

Iago and Cassio enter, Iago still urging Cassio to plead with Desdemona to speak to Othello. But when the ex-lieutenant does so, Desdemona bewails the fact that because of her husband's strange behavior, she has had no real success. Cassio, she says, must be patient; she will do all that she can for him. Iago appears to be amazed at this report; can Othello be *angry?* In mock horror, he cannot believe what he hears: Othello? The even-tempered paragon of perfect control that he has seen on the battlefield? He will go find his general.

Desdemona is convinced that something relating to Othello's public responsibilities or "some unhatch'd practice" (14) – some plot – has seriously disturbed her husband. When Emilia expresses her fervent wish that Othello had not become jealous, the distressed wife states that she has not given him reason to become so. And again the worldly Emilia expresses her cynicism about jealous men, her remark subtly echoing her husband's sarcastic reference to jealousy's being a "green-ey'd monster" (III.iii.166). When Desdemona leaves to find her troubled husband, she says that she will find him and speak further of Cassio's suit. Unhappily, fate could not direct her on a more unwise course.

After the two ladies depart, Bianca, Cassio's mistress, enters and berates her lover for neglecting her bed. Cassio asks to be forgiven and asks the girl to copy the embroidery pattern of a handkerchief he found in his chamber. This becomes a variation of the jealousy theme. The girl suspects that it is "some token from a newer friend" (181) who has replaced her in Cassio's affection. Cassio scoffs at this and mildly upbraids Bianca for becoming jealous without cause. Clearly this is meant to be a miniature mirror of Othello's raging jealousy toward Desdemona. To Bianca, Cassio's admiration of the handkerchief and its unusual embroidery pattern is proof that Cassio loves someone else.

The handkerchief, indeed, seems to have special powers: Othello's mother was convinced it did, as is Othello; Desdemona sang to it, and Iago was so fascinated by it that he insisted that his wife steal it. Cassio too finds it irresistible, and it causes even him misfortune. This thread of the supernatural would especially interest an Elizabethan audience who believed in magic, charms, and even witchcraft. And we should remember that if Brabantio believed that Othello used magical charms to charm Desdemona away from him, we can believe that Desdemona could be persuaded of the magic of this strawberry-embroidered handkerchief.

ACT IV – SCENE 1

Summary

Othello rages and falls into an unconscious trance when Iago tells him that Cassio has admitted that he has lain with Desdemona. Cassio enters, but Iago asks him to withdraw and to return in a short time, since Othello has just suffered an epileptic seizure. Othello recovers and agrees to hide so that he can watch Cassio as Iago draws him out in a conversation about Desdemona. After Cassio's return, Iago engages him in a joking conversation about Bianca's infatuation for him. Othello, who can hear nothing, misinterprets Cassio's laughter and bawdy gestures, believing that they refer to Desdemona. Bianca enters and angrily returns the handkerchief to Cassio, saying that she refuses to copy another woman's present. She leaves, and Cassio follows, trying to appease her. Again, Othello is enraged at this seemingly irrefutable proof of Desdemona's infidelity. At Iago's suggestion, he agrees to strangle Desdemona in her bed; Iago, in turn, promises to murder Cassio.

Lodovico, meanwhile, has arrived on a ship from Venice, bringing a letter from the Duke. He enters with Desdemona. As Othello reads the letter which orders his return to Venice and appoints Cassio as Governor of Cyprus, Desdemona tells Lodovico of the breach between Othello and Cassio. Desdemona's sympathy for Cassio again angers Othello. He strikes her and torments her until she leaves, weeping. Othello, who has not lost all self-control, also leaves. Lodovico is puzzled and saddened.

Commentary

In the first part of this scene, Iago ostensibly tries to comfort Othello; yet, in fact, he continues to torment him with lascivious suggestions of Desdemona's infidelity. He focuses on Othello's confused thoughts as he conjures up visions of Desdemona and Cassio lying naked in bed together; he asks Othello if one can lie thus and "not mean harm" (5). Othello's answer is weighty with irony. The devil, he says, would tempt anyone who would try; as a parallel, consider that the devil (Iago) is at this moment tempting Othello. Othello says further that such lovers "tempt heaven" (8) with damnation; likewise, Othello's irrational actions tempt heaven with the same fate. How successful Iago has been at working toward his own "peculiar end" (I.i.60) is only too clear. Iago knows only too well how deranged his general's mind is; he proclaims that a man and a woman may lie naked together and it would be "a venial slip" (9). But, he exaggerates, if a man gives his wife a *handkerchief* and she . . . He does not even need to finish this illogical, damning conclusion. Othello finishes it himself. He seems to be absolutely within Iago's power. His mind is reeling, and he is easily convinced by Iago's lies that Cassio has boasted of "lying" with Desdemona. Moreover, Othello cannot speak clearly; his thoughts are fragmented as he falls into a trance at Iago's feet, and he is unconscious as Cassio enters and is told by Iago to come back later.

When Othello does revive, he is given no respite from his agony as Iago continues to poison his mind. Sardonically, this newly appointed lieutenant argues that since Othello knows that his wife is unfaithful, his lot is better than the millions of men who are victims of the same deceit and never know about it. Irrationally, Othello can only praise this wisdom of Iago, and as we follow the action in this scene, we watch this tragic hero become almost contemptible because he is so thoroughly the brainwashed dupe of Iago.

As if Othello had not been punished enough by his confused imagination, he allows himself to be hidden by Iago, and Iago promises to talk with Cassio and encourage him to "tell the tale anew,/ Where, how, how oft, how long ago, and when/ He hath, and is again to cope your wife" (85-87). In his soliloquy, Iago reveals the details of this scheme: he will question Cassio about his mistress, Bianca. But the name of Bianca will not be spoken loudly and, therefore, Othello will believe that Cassio will be boasting about his liaison with Desdemona. The scheme works perfectly. Hearing Cassio's raucous laughter, Othello imagines that it is the triumphal laughter of the man who has conquered Desdemona, replaced Othello, and now exults about his latest sexual conquest—Desdemona, who "hangs, and lolls . . . [and] shakes and pulls me" (143-44).

Since Othello continues to listen and does not suddenly challenge Cassio on the spot, we can only conclude that he is transfixed by this revelation and that he is still weak from his nervous collapse. It is apparently for these reasons that he remains still hidden as Bianca enters and haughtily returns the embroidered handkerchief which Cassio gave her to copy. Othello, of course, concludes that this must be the very handkerchief that Iago claims to have seen Cassio wiping his beard with.

When Cassio and Bianca have gone, and Iago is alone, Othello comes forward and his first question speaks volumes: "How shall I murder him, Iago?" (180). He is determined that neither Cassio nor

Desdemona shall live. He would have his wife "rot" (191); he would "hang" (198) her; he will "chop her into messes" (211); he will "poison" (216) her. No punishment is too severe for one who has allegedly betrayed Othello's love, his reputation, and his pride.

Iago cannot wait for his general to decide how he will kill Desdemona; he himself means to "enmesh [ensnare] them all" (II.iii.368), and the sooner the better. Obtaining poison, he knows, is no problem, but it might not work, and Desdemona's death *must* be accomplished quickly – while Othello's passion is at a high pitch. For this reason, he orders Othello to "strangle her in her bed . . . the bed she hath contaminated" (220-21). Iago, meanwhile, will kill Cassio.

Othello's fury seems almost totally unsympathetic at this point. He is so very wrong, so devoid of reason. Yet Shakespeare depicts him as a man for whom we can still feel a measure of pity. We can never forget that Othello has been corrupted by a master fiend, and we must not overlook one of Othello's key lines: "But yet the pity of it, Iago! O Iago, the pity of it, Iago!" (206-7)

When Lodovico, Desdemona, and several attendants enter, Othello's words and actions would not seem so incredible if Shakespeare had not prepared us so well. Lodovico is a kinsman of the aristocratic Brabantio and has arrived here as an emissary from the Venetian senate. His cordial welcome to Othello ("[God] Save you, worthy General") is unknowingly ominous and also ironic; only God, in fact, can save Othello now and the "worthy General" is soon to dispel all such notions about himself and his worthiness. Yet Othello does recover himself sufficiently to take care of the immediate amenities, and while he reads the letter from the Venetian senate, Lodovico asks about Lieutenant Cassio. It is Iago who answers, and his answer is portentous; his brief statement that Cassio "lives" (286) includes an unsaid "still" – that is, Othello has ordered Iago to kill the Florentine within three hours.

Desdemona's reaction to Lodovico's question is swift; she describes the division between Othello and Cassio and expresses her hope "t'atone them, for the love I bear to Cassio" (244). Emilia's comments about jealous men and about Othello's earlier, unreasonable jealousy seem to be forgotten. Desdemona's answer to Lodovico is openly naive, as is her reaction to her husband's anger. The mere mention of Cassio's name, of course, is enough to inflame the Moor. Not only does he publicly berate Desdemona as a devil, but he strikes her and orders her out of his sight. When Lodovico asks Othello to call Desdemona back, he does so, answering Lodovico cooly that, concerning the senate's letter, he acknowledges that he is called back, commanded home, and will return to Venice; at the same time, he mutters in a countertempo disgusting insults about Desdemona.

He then agrees that Cassio shall have his place; remember, in this respect, that he mistakenly believes that Cassio has already taken his place in Desdemona's bed. The Moor's official welcome to Lodovico is given an added flourish; he welcomes him "to Cyprus. – Goats and monkeys!" (274) This is an allusion to the bestial, carnal imagery which Iago used earlier to suggest Desdemona and Cassio's copulation.

Lodovico finds Othello's conduct inexcusable; he is stunned by the actions of the "noble Moor" (III.iv.26), the man whose character "passion cannot shake" (IV.i.277), whose "solid virtue" (IV.i.277) has always had a reputation for being invincible. These, remember, are the virtues which were used to describe Othello before Iago began his evil machinations. Othello has permitted passion to "shake" him; it has destroyed his "solid virtue." In a word, he has not survived the supreme test which a hero in high tragedy must undergo.

As the two men conclude the scene with a brief bit of dialogue, Iago speaks to Lodovico and seems to be much aggrieved. His comment that Othello "is much chang'd" (279) is a most effective, but despicable understatement. To the emissary from Venice, as to all others, Iago seems cool, honest, concerned, fair, and trustworthy – noble, even.

ACT IV – SCENE 2

Summary

Questioned by Othello, Emilia swears that Desdemona is chaste. Othello then sends for Desdemona and asks her to swear that she has been faithful. She does so, but Othello will not believe her. He accuses her of being a whore and a strumpet. When he leaves, Desdemona sends for Iago and asks him how she can clear herself. Iago tells her to be calm and patient: the fault is not in her; perhaps an official matter has temporarily disturbed Othello. Desdemona and Emilia leave as Roderigo enters. Iago has convinced him that Cassio must be killed, and together they plot the murder.

Commentary

In this scene, Emilia redeems herself somewhat; earlier, she had an opportunity to speak out in defense of Desdemona and correct Othello's jealous insinuations, but she did not do so. Now, alone with her, he questions her specifically regarding the behavior of his wife, and he insinuates that, being a good friend of Desdemona's, she has surely observed Desdemona in compromising situations. Emilia's answer is firm; she has never seen anything improper nor heard anything that would make her suspect that Desdemona has been less than faithful. Yes, she has seen Desdemona and Cassio together, but she stresses that she has heard "each syllable" (5) that has been uttered between them. In addition, they have never whispered together nor did they send her out on any unnecessary errands so that they might be alone. Emilia would "lay down [her] soul at stake" (13) on Desdemona's chastity. She curses the "wretch . . . [who] put this in your head" (15); unknowingly, she curses her own husband. Othello is not convinced. At this point, his opinion of women is less than Emilia's opinion of men; Iago, we should realize, is responsible for his wife's cynicism about men, and he is also responsible for Othello's condemnation of women and of Desdemona, in particular. Thus when Othello asks Emilia for her opinion of Desdemona's fidelity, he gives her answer little credence. He sums up Emilia as "a simple bawd" (20) and his own wife as a "subtle whore" (21), secretive and hypocritical.

Parenthetically, perhaps it should be noted that Shakespeare was not as careful about his time element in this play as he was when he created his magnificent characterizations. For example, if we are to try to fathom Othello's changes of character and pity his dissolution, we must believe that sufficient time and opportunity has elapsed for Cassio to have actually engaged in an affair with Desdemona. In actuality, however, there has been no such time available, and it is impossible for Bianca to berate Cassio for neglecting her for at least a week. But such minor flaws as these must be overlooked. Shakespeare knew what he was doing. Rapidity of movement is necessary to attain dramatic tension, and because Othello insists on establishing Desdemona's infidelity, we must concentrate on the psychology of the man which has been perverted by Iago, and we must not be unduly concerned about the actual clock time elapsed.

When Desdemona is brought to Othello, he puts her through a cruel ordeal of questions and accusations, concluding that she is a whore and ignoring her protestations. First, he melodramatically hurries Emilia out of the room, asking her to "stand guard" and warn them [the "procreants" (28)] if anyone comes; by using the term "procreants," Othello suggests that he and Desdemona need a few stolen minutes to have sex together. This is a travesty of how they might act if they were illicit lovers. When they are alone, Othello demands uncompromisingly that Desdemona swear to heaven that she is "honest" (38), which she does, and after which Othello feels satisfied that when he kills her, as he certainly means to do, he will be striking down one who blasphemes against heaven. Meanwhile, Desdemona, in her innocence, cannot believe that her fidelity – or infidelity – is at the root of her husband's behavior. She grasps for reasons, believing that perhaps Othello is punishing her because her father has recalled him to Venice. Perhaps to disguise a professional disappointment to his honor, Othello is punishing her because in his anger and frustration he must punish *someone.*

In a word, Desdemona is stunned as her once-noble husband can no longer hold back his tears. Othello regains himself, however, and at line 47, he begins an eighteen-line soliloquy in which Shakespeare restores an aura of the tragic hero to the Moor. This is great poetry, and here once again we view the high-minded Othello, a man who is capable of uttering magnificent concepts in language that carries its own sense of majesty. Notice, for example, the tacit reference to the afflictions of Job (48-49) and the broad range of imagery which expresses so clearly and movingly the turmoil in a man whose paradise is lost. The image of "a cistern for foul toads" (61), with its emphasis on gross sensuality, is followed by the startling vision of "patience, thou young and rose-lipp'd cherubin" (63). Such poetry contains keen visual oppositions of figurative language and reveals the almost unbearable tension in Othello and the sudden change that has taken place in him.

After the Moor's exit, we see the change that has taken place in Desdemona. As Emilia endeavors to comfort her mistress, she is told in a few words that Othello is no longer Desdemona's "lord" (102), and that Desdemona is too distressed even to cry, for she is at a total and complete loss to understand the unfathomable change in her husband's character. There is a faint trace of feyness and madness in this scene, as though Desdemona were speaking with a glazed countenance. Even Emilia notes this change when her mistress asks that her wedding sheets be laid out on her bed (105-6) and asks that Iago be brought to her.

When Iago enters, Desdemona cannot bring herself to utter the actual slanderous abuses which Othello has heaped upon her; this is further proof of her bewilderment. Our focus then moves to Emilia. While Othello is raging somewhere else in the castle and Desdemona is numbed and Iago is wailing in mock horror at what has happened, Emilia stands back and expresses her conviction that "some eternal villain,/ Some busy and insinuating rogue,/ Some cogging, cozening slave" (130-32), ambitious "to get some office" (132) has slandered Desdemona. Her insight is remarkably on target. Ironically, it is not Desdemona who has been seduced; it is Othello whose sanity has been victimized by "some most villainous knave,/ Some base notorious knave" (139-40). Emilia curses any man who would label Desdemona a whore, reminding Iago (and us) that Desdemona is a strong woman who defied "her father and her country and her friends" (126) for the man she loved. Desdemona is an extraordinary woman who could have married any number of Venetian men but she chose Othello and thereby gave her total, undivided allegiance to him, a man of another race and of another country.

When Desdemona pleads with Iago to tell her how she may win back the trust and love of Othello, we realize that this is a dark parallel to the incident that initiated Desdemona's plight. Earlier, Cassio asked her to speak to Othello and effect a reconciliation; now Desdemona asks Iago to speak to Othello and effect a reconciliation. In both cases, Iago is the villain who is responsible for the breach of love.

The scene ends as Iago once more dupes the gullible Roderigo; this time he dupes him into killing Cassio so that he can ostensibly win Desdemona's favors more easily. We also learn what mischief Iago has been into while offstage. We learn, for example, that he has pocketed enough jewels (meant for Desdemona) to "have corrupted a votarist [a nun]" (192). Finally, Roderigo is beginning to believe that he has been swindled. He knows that his advances toward Desdemona are not right – and he is ready to cease them, but he wants his jewels back. The quick-thinking Iago, however, diverts him for the time being. Again proving that he is the tactician who can nimbly improvise as he traces his path of villainy, Iago has another plan by which he convinces Roderigo that he might yet gain Desdemona's favors. The visiting commission from Venice plans to appoint Cassio to replace

Othello in Cyprus, says Iago; if that happens, Desdemona will leave with her husband. But if a man of "mettle" (207) – Roderigo – were to kill Cassio ("knocking out his brains") (236), then Othello and Desdemona would have to stay on. Cassio will be dining tonight with a harlot and will probably leave between twelve and one. Roderigo can kill him then, and Iago promises to be nearby "to second [the] attempt" (244). The plan is irresistible to Roderigo.

ACT IV – SCENE 3

Summary

Othello orders Desdemona to go to bed unattended; she agrees to do so, and as Emilia prepares her friend for bed, Desdemona's mind wanders, preoccupied with sad thoughts. She sings the "Willow Song," a song she learned from her mother's maid, a woman who loved a man who went mad. In contrast to Emilia and her worldly opinions, Desdemona swears that she could never dishonor her husband – for any price.

Commentary

Desdemona's superior breeding is evident in the early part of this scene. She has sufficiently recovered herself and has presided as the hostess at a dinner for Lodovico and the other members of the commission from Venice; following that, when Othello expresses the desire to walk alone with Lodovico, she submits to her husband's dismissal. She seems exhausted and does not protest his ordering her to bed or even his ordering her to dismiss Emilia.

Emilia, in contrast, is resentful of Othello's behavior and deeply concerned about her friend. Othello's commands do not intimidate her; she wishes that Desdemona had "never seen him!" (18). But Desdemona, not even in her unhappiness, has no such wish. Her love "doth so approve him/ . . . even his stubbornness" (19-20). This is the man of her choice, despite his roughness and rebukes, and when her wedding sheets are laid out, as she has asked Emilia to do, she announces in words that are strongly prophetic: "If I do die before, prithee, shroud me/ In one of those same sheets" (24-25); it is apparent that Desdemona has a premonition of her own death. She then tells Emilia how she came to learn the mournful "Willow Song"; it was sung by poor Barbary, her mother's maid, whose lover went mad and deserted her.

Rather oddly, it seems, Shakespeare inserts a brief reference to Lodovico here; Desdemona praises him as a man who "speaks well" (37). Emilia is no less approving in her remarks. Exactly what Shakespeare intended here is hard to imagine; perhaps, for the moment, the young wife feels abandoned and is comparing her moody, raging Moor with the Venetians she once knew.

The "Willow Song" is an old one, existing in many versions before Shakespeare incorporated it into his play. Of special interest is line 52 which echoes, as it were, Desdemona's thoughts in lines 19-20 – that is, in the song, it is the male lover who is false and the cause of the poor woman's sighing and weeping. Obviously the mood perfectly reflects that of Desdemona, whose love is so strong that she approves Othello's frowns, just as the "poor soul" (41) in the song approves her lover's "scorn" (52).

Othello's unfair accusations have undone Desdemona; she asks Emilia if, truthfully, there are "women [who] do abuse their husbands/ In such gross kind?" (62-63). The idea is unthinkable for Desdemona; "by this heavenly light" (65), she swears that she could never make love with another man. Emilia lightens the tenseness of this moment by remarking that she would never betray Iago in "this heavenly light" – that is, she herself prefers to make love in the dark. Emilia, as noted, has no illusions about men or love or marriage vows. Illicit sex is a small vice; of course she would cheat on her husband – but not for a trifle. Like most women, Emilia would make a cuckold of her husband if it would make him a monarch. In fact, she would tempt purgatory if there were sufficient cause. Unfaithful wives are many, she says, and she blames husbands for their wives' loose behavior, insisting that women should have a right to do whatever men do. Since they can't, however, they must avenge themselves upon their wayward husbands. A wife should not be judged nor treated with less respect than a man – that is Emilia's firm dictum. She spurns the double standard that justifies a man's actions – right or wrong – and condemns the same acts when done by a woman. Clearly, she speaks from her years of living as Iago's wife. Too long has she seen his hypocrisy and his faults which she – a woman – would be censored for committing. The purpose of all this chatter, of course, is to keep before us the theme of infidelity.

The mood changes, and with Desdemona's short prayer that she should never be guilty of returning evil for evil, she says goodnight to her friend. The contrast between Desdemona's young innocence and the worldliness of Emilia intensifies our pity for the young bride as she prepares for bed and for Othello's return.

ACT V – SCENE 1

Summary

Late that same night on a street in Cyprus, Iago and Roderigo are waiting for an opportunity to murder Cassio. As Cassio enters, Roderigo's thrust at him fails and, instead, *Roderigo* is wounded. Iago then darts out from where he is hiding, wounds Cassio in the leg, then exits. Othello, passing by, hears Cassio cry out the word "Murder!" and believes that Iago's plot has been successful. Lodovico and Gratiano enter and, after them, Iago comes onstage with a light. Both wounded men are still alive; Iago comforts Cassio and then surreptitiously stabs Roderigo in the darkness. Bianca enters, and Iago tries to implicate her since Cassio just dined with her. Cassio and Roderigo are carried off. Emilia enters, and Iago sends her to tell Othello what has occurred.

Commentary

In this scene, which precedes the final and climactic one, Shakespeare provides exciting physical action. Iago gives Roderigo final instructions for slaying Cassio; this is the moment of crisis, he says; this "makes us, or it mars us" (4), and he urges his rich, gullible friend to be firm in his resolution. Roderigo, however, is hardly a model of determination and confidence, and Iago finds it necessary to strongly reassure him. For his part, Roderigo is not eager to commit murder and he gives some evidence of a twinge of conscience before concluding " 'tis but a man gone" (10). In an aside, Iago voices his thoughts: both Roderigo and Cassio are sources of displeasure to him. He gains if one is slain, and he gains even more if both are slain. If Roderigo survives this confrontation, Iago has not yet determined how he will explain the pawned jewels; if Roderigo is killed and Cassio lives, Iago has another problem: this Florentine is young, handsome and well-mannered, and Iago cuts a poor figure next to him. There is also the possibility that the Moor might eventually discover how Iago arrang-ed to have Cassio killed and could, presumably, "unfold [the plan] to him" (21).

Cassio enters and is set upon, but Roderigo's sword is stopped by the young man's coat of mail. Thereupon, Cassio draws his sword and wounds Roderigo, who cries out that he is slain. At this crucial moment, Iago darts out from behind Cassio, severely wounds him in the leg and disappears into the night. Othello enters and hears Cassio crying, "Murder! Murder!" He believes that Iago has carried out his vow: Cassio is dead.

Because of the darkness, Othello mistakes Roderigo for Iago and praises him as "honest and just" (31); Iago's prompt execution of revenge convinces Othello that his lieutenant has done his duty and, satisfied, he leaves without examining Cassio any further. He is now more anxious than ever to find his "strumpet" (34) in her "bed, lust-stain'd" (36); when he is finished, both she and Cassio "shall with lust's blood be spotted" (36). He exits quickly, just before Lodovico and Gratiano enter. Both men hear Cassio's outcries and Roderigo's anguished curse against the man who has wounded him.

Iago enters with a light, much to Lodovico's delight. He welcomes help, especially that of the "very valiant" (52) Iago. Cassio is likewise relieved and tells Iago that villains have attacked him. In the melee, Iago is able to get to Roderigo's side and fatally stab him, then cry out sanctimoniously against men who kill in the dark. This done, he calls Lodovico's attention to the wounded Cassio as he bends down, tears off his shirt, and begins to bind up Cassio's wounds.

When Bianca enters, she breaks into sobs – to which Iago reacts with scorn, casting immediate suspicion on her, a "notable strumpet" (78). He calls for a garter to use as a tourniquet, then tells them all that he suspects "this trash/ To be a party in this injury" (85-86). On seeing Roderigo's corpse, he pretends great surprise to find his "friend and . . . dear countryman" (88). He continues to busy himself with Cassio's wound, getting him into a chair, and apologizing to Gratiano for this terrible unpleasantness. To Cassio, he inquires about "these bloody accidents" (94). Cassio, of course, has no answers; he doesn't even know Roderigo or why the man would want to kill him.

This scene belongs to Iago. His masterly handling of the bungled murder, his cool villainy as he stabs Roderigo, and his attending to Cassio are accomplished with superb finesse. Fate even offers Iago the frightened, silent Bianca, at whom he can contemptuously point a finger of guilt as he calls Lodovico and Gratiano's attention to "the gastness [ghastliness] of her eye" (106). "Guiltiness," Iago announces, will have a way of revealing itself, even though "tongues [are] out of use" (109-10).

Emilia arrives and learns of Cassio's wound and Roderigo's death, much to her genuine sorrow. Iago, of course, takes advantage of all this to voice more sanctimonious words and to repeat his false suspicions regarding Bianca. It will be noted that Emilia still finds no reason not to believe that her husband is basically "honest," in respect to this particular violence.

The scene ends as Iago sends his wife to inform Othello and Desdemona what has happened. Alone, he acknowledges the fact that his success or failure will be determined this very night, a clear indication that the resolution of the entire action is close at hand.

ACT V – SCENE 2

Summary

Desdemona is nearly asleep in her bed chamber as Othello enters. He extinguishes his candle and, filled with regret, he gives her a last kiss. Desdemona awakens and, realizing her husband's intent, pleads for mercy. But Othello will not be stopped and he smothers her. Emilia pounds at the door, trying to bring news of Cassio, but Othello does not let her in to deliver Iago's message until Desdemona is apparently dead.

Emilia enters and discovers Desdemona's body; then she hears her friend faintly moaning, trying to hide Othello's guilt. Othello, however, confesses the murder, saying that it was Iago who convinced him that Desdemona was a strumpet. Horrified, Emilia tells him that Iago has told him lies; she then rushes out to announce the crime. Montano, Gratiano, Iago, and the others enter. Othello begins to tell of his suspicions, based upon the handkerchief, and Emilia, realizing her part in all this, confesses that it was she who found the handkerchief and gave it to Iago. Infuriated, Iago kills Emilia as Othello is disarmed by Montano. Othello manages to find another sword and wounds Iago for his deception. Little by little, the full circumstances are exposed. In complete despair over Desdemona's death, Othello stabs himself with a concealed dagger as the others look on in horror. Othello dies, kissing his young wife.

Commentary

Desdemona is asleep in her bed as Othello enters, carrying a candle. He is no longer the angry, vengeful husband. His soliloquy is quiet, and he seems to be more an agent of justice than the jealous cuckold. He speaks repeatedly of "the cause . . . the cause" (1) — that is, Desdemona's unchastity, and he himself even hesitates to speak aloud the name of Desdemona's crime before the "chaste stars" (2). At last, Othello assumes the posture of the tragic hero, grossly wrong in his determination, yet steeling himself to do what he must. Here is what remains of the Othello of earlier acts — a man admirably self-possessed, the master of the situation. In this soliloquy there are no references to strumpets or whores, nor to coupling goats or monkeys, nor to any other images which once racked him with jealousy. No longer is he possessed with revenge for his grievously injured pride. But there remains a passionate conviction of righteousness in his words — despite his monumental error. He is convinced that he is being merciful in performing a deed which must be done. Thus he will not shed Desdemona's blood (instead, he will smother her); nor will he scar her physical beauty; nor would he, as we learn later, kill her *soul*. Yet he *will* kill her; Desdemona must die; "else she'll betray more men" (6). And there is devastating irony as he says, "Put out the light, and then put out the light" (7); Desdemona was once the "light" of his life and, also, light is often equated in Elizabethan dramas with reason, especially right reason, the aim of all men. Here, however, Othello means to act righteously, but he fails to use his sense of logic or reason; he has condemned Desdemona without proof, without reason. He is torn between his love for her (evidenced by his kiss) and his resolve to cooly execute justice. Desdemona is a "pattern of excelling nature" (11), yet she is also "cunning" (11). He compares her to a rose which, once plucked, can bloom no more and must wither. For a moment, his love for her almost persuades "justice" (meaning Othello) "to break [his] sword" (17). He weeps, but he regains his purpose; Desdemona's beauty is deceptive, he realizes, because it masks her corruption.

When Othello's words awaken Desdemona, she begins an agonizing attempt to reason with her husband. The Moor then urges her to pray for forgiveness of any sin within her soul, and she becomes increasingly terrified. This he mistakenly concludes to be additional evidence of her guilt. He is as convinced of this as she is convinced that Othello is absolutely serious about killing her. Logically, she knows that she should have no cause for fear – she has done no wrong – yet she fears her husband. Othello is not moved in the least by her insistence that she did not give the handkerchief to Cassio. And it is notable throughout this harrowing episode that Othello's language is controlled and elevated. As Desdemona cries out, first for heaven to have mercy on her and later for the Lord Himself to have mercy on her, Othello voices a solemn "amen" to her prayers and addresses her as a "sweet soul" (50). But even now he refuses to see her as anything but a "perjur'd woman" (63) (a lying woman), one who forces him "to do/ A murder" (64-65). At this moment, the motive of personal revenge surfaces again within him and replaces controlled justice. His resolve of self-control breaks when Desdemona calls out for Cassio; he is convinced that he indeed heard Cassio laughing about a sexual liaison with Desdemona. When Desdemona hears that Iago has killed Cassio, her self-control likewise vanishes. She pleads for her life, asking for banishment, asking for at least a day's stay in her execution, at least half a day, but she is overpowered by the Moor. He smothers her as she begs to say one last prayer.

It is at this moment that Emilia arrives outside the door, crying loudly for Othello. The Moor does not answer immediately. From his words, we realize that he is convinced that he is being merciful, if cruel, and that he intends to be sure that his wife is dead. The monstrosity of what he has done overwhelms him. Significant are lines 100-102, in which he says that there should be now "a huge eclipse/ Of sun and moon" – that is, some evidence in the heavens that should acknowledge that Desdemona is dead.

Again, Emilia calls out to Othello and, on entering, she shrieks about "foul murders" (106). Othello fears she is right and blames the moon, which "makes men mad" (111). It is then that he learns that Cassio lives, and he hears Desdemona's weak voice. Once more the young wife proclaims her innocence and insists that no one but herself is to blame. Indeed, she jeopardizes her very soul by deliberately lying in order to protect Othello, her husband, to whom she asks to be commended.

At first, Othello denies having any part in his wife's death. But then he loudly denounces her as a "liar, gone to burning hell" (129), admitting that he killed her. "She turn'd to folly, and she was a whore" (132); "she was false as water . . . Cassio did top her" (134-36). His proof is "honest, honest Iago" (154). Without hesitation, Emilia denounces Iago as a liar and Othello as a deceived "dolt" (163). She defies Othello's sword to right the injustice of this murder, vowing to "make thee known/ Though I lost twenty lives" (165-66) and crying out for help, proclaiming that Othello has murdered Desdemona.

When Montano, Gratiano, and the others enter, Emilia challenges her husband to disprove what Othello has told her. In response to her pointed questions, Iago concedes that he did report that Desdemona was unfaithful, but that Othello himself found the same to be true. Summoning new courage, Emilia ignores her husband's command to be quiet and go home. Imploring the others to hear her, she curses Iago and prophetically states that perhaps she will never go home (197). All this finally becomes unbearable for the Moor, and he falls upon his wife's bed, only to be mocked by Emilia for his anguish. Gratiano then speaks and tells us that he finds comfort in the fact that Desdemona's father is not alive to hear of this tragedy; already he is dead of grief because of Desdemona's marrying the Moor. This is news we are not aware of, and it makes Desdemona's innocence and her deep love for Othello even more poignant.

Othello insists here that "Iago knows" (210) and, as further proof, he speaks of the handkerchief. At the mention of this, Emilia cries out again, this time appealing to God: no one will stop her now. She pays no attention to Iago's drawn sword as she tells how she found the handkerchief and gave it to Iago; she repeats her claim, even though Iago denounces her as a "villainous whore" (229) and a "liar" (231).

Thus the full truth is unfolded for Othello. He dashes toward Iago, is disarmed by Montano, and in the confusion, Iago kills Emilia, then flees. All leave, except the dying Emilia and the Moor, who can only berate himself. Emilia, aware that she is near death, recalls Desdemona's prophetic "Willow Song," a bit of which she sings. She reaffirms the innocence of her mistress just before she dies and concludes: "She lov'd thee, cruel Moor" (249).

Othello finds one of his prized weapons, a Spanish sword, and, in a soliloquy, he recalls that he used the sword boldly in the past. Now, however, he has come to his "journey's end" (267). He sees himself as a lost soul ("where should Othello go?") (271)). He is a "cursed slave" (276) who deserves the worst of punishment.

Lodovico, Montano, Iago (a prisoner now) and several officers enter; Cassio, in a chair, is brought in. The final moment of revelation is at hand. Othello lunges at Iago, wounds him, and is disarmed. Death is too good for Iago, he says; " 'tis happiness to die" (290). Death is a relief he would not offer to his archenemy. When Cassio states quietly that he never gave the Moor reason to distrust him, Othello readily accepts his word and asks for his pardon. Othello is freshly aware that he has been ensnared body and soul by "that demi-devil" (301) Iago, who refuses to confess his villainy. Lodovico then produces two letters found on Roderigo's body: one tells of the plan to slay Cassio, and the other is Roderigo's denunciation of Iago. The details of how Cassio obtained the handkerchief are revealed, and Othello bewails the fact that he has been a "fool! fool! fool!" (323).

Lodovico vows to punish Iago and tells Othello that he must return with him to Venice. Othello acknowledges the sentence, but before he is led away, he speaks his final lines. Unmistakably he has recovered his basic nobility and that gift of impressive language which he commanded so well prior to Iago's temptation. He reminds his listeners of his past service to the Venetian state and pleads that his story shall be reported accurately so that all will know him *not* as a barbarous foreigner but as one who "lov'd not wisely but too well" (334), as one who was preyed upon and became "perplex'd in the extreme" (346) and "threw a pearl away/ Richer than all his tribe" (347-48). We should not overlook this simile; Othello compares himself to the "base Judean" who threw away the most valuable pearl in the world. Relentless in his self-reproach, Othello tacitly compares himself to "a malignant and a turban'd Turk" (353); then, finished, he stabs himself in an attempt to atone for all that has happened. He himself chooses to execute the necessary justice upon himself. As he is dying, he says that he kissed Desdemona before he killed her. This suggests that perhaps his love for her flickered briefly within his dark soul before he murdered her. He reminds himself that perhaps he was not wholly corrupt, but he dies knowing that his soul is lost.

Lodovico's sad words end the tragedy. The sight of Othello, slumped against Desdemona's bed, "poisons sight" (364). He asks for the curtains to be drawn, for Gratiano to administer the Moor's estate, and for Iago to be punished. He must return to Venice and "with heavy heart" (371) relate "this heavy act" (371).

CHARACTER ANALYSES

Othello

As the foremost officer in the state of Venice and as the new Governor-General of Cyprus, Othello is clearly a general in rank. He is sometimes, however, referred to as "captain." This confusion was not unusual in Elizabethan times, since "captain" was a term also applied to a general, a survival from Roman times. But there was a more important Elizabethan reason for this dual use of terms. Generals, however exalted their status, usually also kept the proud title of "captain" of a company. This was their basic and permanent rank. Othello is thus both a captain and a general. He is, likewise, a mercenary. It was the practice of some Italian city-states to employ a remarkably capable foreigner as the head of their army.

Othello possesses all the virtues for a general prescribed by Renaissance military treatises. He is of noble birth; he is self-controlled; he is religious; he has the respect of his men; and he demonstrates the most advanced Renaissance military knowledge in choosing for his lieutenant a man (Cassio) versed in military science – rather than one (Iago) who has proved himself only as a good combat soldier. This choice provokes deep resentment by Iago in the opening scene and is the reason for his contemptuously caustic reference to Cassio as "the bookish theoric" (I.i.24).

As with most of Shakespeare's tragic heroes, Othello is magnified and ennobled; in Act I, Scene 3, he identifies himself with the "great ones" of the world – and he does so without the slightest show of arrogance. He is, as it were, "larger than life." His magnetism is what draws the allegiance and awe of the Venetian senators and soldiers alike and what absolutely captivates Desdemona. Likewise, Othello's jealousy is not of the pale sort. The Moor towers in sheer force and nobility above all others in Venice, and from first to last, he is aware of his high position. This is what makes his final realization of how unjust he has been so tragic.

To show us that Othello is an outstanding example of an able military man and a courageous leader, Shakespeare initially has one of the senators in Act I, Scene 3, remark: "Here comes Brabantio and the valiant Moor" (47). Then, as Othello, Brabantio, Cassio, Iago, Roderigo, and others enter, the Duke of Venice says, "Valiant Othello, we must straight employ you/ Against the general enemy Ottoman"

(48-49). This is merely the first of a series of comments by various characters attesting to Othello's courage and ability as a warrior. And a point that is rarely mentioned, but one that is important in any discussion of Othello is the fact that he has been a soldier since he was seven years old! – ". . . since these arms of mine had seven years' pith . . . they have us'd/ Their dearest action in the tented field" (I.iii.83-85). Othello, thus, is no mere newcomer to the battlefield. The life and customs of the soldier are what he is used to, and to him war is a proud and glorious way of life. Another seemingly insignificant but telling remark about Othello's soldierly courage occurs in Act II, Scene 1; an unidentified gentleman on the seacoast, anxiously awaiting the safe arrival of Othello's ship, realizes that Cassio's ship has safely docked and notes that Cassio is the lieutenant "to the warlike Moor Othello" (27). Montano, Governor of Cyprus, is likewise on the seacoast and says that he has "serv'd him [Othello], and the man commands/ Like a full soldier" (35-36); later, he adds, in admiration, another word of praise: "brave Othello" (38).

In addition to Othello's soldierly courage, he exhibits great dignity and self-control – that is, before Iago poisons his mind with jealousy. Also in the first act, Othello refuses to be alarmed by Iago's account of the wrath of Brabantio. "Let him do his spite," the Moor says; "My services which I have done the signiory/ Shall out-tongue his complaints" (17-19). Othello knows, modestly but surely, his worth. Later, Othello refuses to retreat before Brabantio's men: "My parts, my title, and my perfect soul/ Shall manifest me rightly" (31-32). And still later in the same act and scene (I.ii), Othello remains calm in the face of Brabantio's swordsmen and even gracious to his new father-in-law: "Keep up your bright swords, for the dew will rust them," the Moor jests; "Good signior [Brabantio], you shall more command with years/ Than with your weapons" (59-61). Othello's perfect confidence in himself makes others look lesser in comparison. His patience with Brabantio's charge of witchcraft (I.iii.76) is admirably restrained: "Most potent, grave, and reverend signiors . . ." prefaces his defense, and this discipline is a significant contrast to Brabantio's near-hysteria.

The breakdown of Othello's remarkable self-control occurs perhaps first in Act III, Scene 3. Othello is so consumed with anger and jealousy-that one might almost expect him to seize Iago by the throat when he challenges Iago to prove Desdemona's infidelity. There is no textual indication of any physical violence, however; in lines

359-60, Othello says simply, but fiercely, "Villain, be sure thou prove my love a whore;/ Be sure of it. Give me the ocular proof." In other words, report to me what you actually see with your own eyes. This is a contrast to Desdemona's defending her husband's perfect self-control to the dubious Emilia in Act III, Scene 4; she refers to Othello as "my noble Moor" (26) and says that he "is true of mind and made of no such baseness/ As jealous creatures are . . ." (26-28).

Yet the sad dissemination of Othello's once renowned dignity and self-control does occur, and this is especially potent in Act IV, Scene 1. Othello has been unusually abrasive to Desdemona, and Lodovico makes a definitive comment on the change in his old friend: "Is this the nature/ Whom passion could not shake?" (276-77).

Basically, one of the first qualities that comes to mind when one assesses a man as complex as Othello is his openness — his trustfulness, in short. Speaking of Iago, his "ancient," an Elizabethan term for an aide-de-camp, or ensign, Othello says that Iago is a man of honesty and trust; "to his conveyance I assign my wife" (I.iii.286). Othello has no reason to distrust Iago at this point; it is evident that he also trusts his wife, since he assigns her to the care of another man. The absence of any sexual jealousy here makes Othello's later breakdown even more striking and poignant. Later in the same act and scene, Brabantio suggests that Desdemona deceived *him* and may just as easily deceive Othello, and Othello's reply is markedly significant: "My life upon her faith!" (295). His faith in Desdemona is not only dramatically important for the later, tragic reversal, but significant here because of its obvious actuality. He deeply loves and trusts his young and beautiful wife, despite the fact that he is an aging man and might be expected, normally, to be a little suspicious of — if not his wife — of other men. And he is not. In fact, Othello's "free and open nature" (Iago's own summation of his general) is the very reason that Othello is such an easy prey for Iago. Iago knows that Othello is, by nature, neither overly introspective nor overly interested in the motivations of others.

Time after time, Othello fails to see through the machinations of Iago. Othello trusts too easily. Iago is a military man; Othello is used to dealing with men on the battlefield, men whom he must trust and, moreover, Iago has a well-known reputation for honesty. Othello needs to trust people; it is his nature; that is why he suffers such terrible agony when he must try to choose between the alleged honesty of Iago and the honesty of Desdemona. Desperately, Othello *needs* to trust his wife; in Act III, Scene 3, he cries, "If she be false, O, then heaven mocks itself!/ I'll not believe 't" (278-79). This is overwhelming evidence that he does *need* to believe *her*, just as in many of his other speeches, there are similar, parallel expressions of his *need* to believe *Iago*. At this particular point in the play, Othello has not become "evil"; there seems to be no jealousy nor even any seeing it in other people. This comes later – and very soon.

Othello's inclination to trust Iago is easily perceived, as we have already noted ("The Moor already changes with my poison" (III.iii.325)). Iago almost assumes here the role of a Frankenstein-kind of doctor, creating and delighting in the making of a monster. And our hearts respond greatly to the final breakdown of Othello's once-ordered existence as he desperately clings to the one thing that seems certain to him: Iago's sincere friendship: "O brave Iago, honest and just,/ Thou hast such noble sense . . ." (V.i.31-32).

This "innocence" of Othello – that is, this simple directness of character that is so dominant an element of his personality is a facet which one should always consider. Particularly should one note his "innocence" early in the play, perhaps best evidenced in Act I, Scene 3, when Othello, defending himself against Brabantio's ravings, says quietly and simply that he is "rude" (meaning "unpolished," "simple," or "unsophisticated") in his speech, and that he is not "bless'd with the soft phrase of peace" (82); clearly, he does not try to posture or assume a pose that might seem weighty or overly impressive; it would be unnatural and fraudulent for such a man as Othello. This early example of the Moor's "innocence" is a necessary foil to the play's abundance of intrigue. And, as has been noted, Othello tells his version of his wooing of Desdemona "unvarnish'd" (90). Truthfully, he points out to the Duke that Desdemona's father "lov'd [him]" (I.iii.128) and questioned him often about his adventurous life. Straightforwardly in the same scene, Othello confesses, "This only is the witchcraft I have us'd" (169). This innocence is touching; Othello truly believes that it was the spell of his tales alone that won over not only Desdemona, but also her father.

Othello, tragically, in Act III, Scene 3, in a moment of rashness even cries out for an innocence that is an innocence far different from what we have just discussed. Thoroughly corrupted at this point by Iago's poison, Othello deeply desires the innocence of the "unthinking man"—that is, he would rather have had his entire company of soldiers have had sex with Desdemona—if he could have remained innocent of the knowledge that such a bizarre incident had occurred.

But Othello's "innocence" is shattered, as are his other esteemed qualities by Iago, and this is pointedly evident in the same act and the same scene (III.iii) when he says that he thinks that Desdemona is honest and, yet, he thinks that she is not. He does not know what to believe anymore. This is painful. Othello, once a master of self-knowledge has been reduced to a trembling, helpless tool of the evil Iago.

In addition to this play's being a tragedy of multiple dimensions, it is also a love story—the tale of a man who loved excessively but "lov'd not wisely" (V.ii.346). Numerous instances of Othello's love for Desdemona have been noted and quoted already, but a few lines deserve special recognition because of their exquisite, sensitive poetry and relevance. In Act II, Scene 1, Othello exults, "O my soul's joy!/ If after every tempest come such calms . . ." (186-87). This passage needs to be noted because it is a bit different from the effusiveness that Othello so often expresses for Desdemona. Here, he evidences both the ardor and potential violence of his love. And, a few lines later, he says, "If it were now to die,/ 'Twere now to be most happy . . ." (191-92). This speech is beautiful and heartfelt and is clear-cut proof for the audience of his deep, sincere love for his young bride. In addition, the speech should be noted because of Shakespeare's embellishing it with the ironic overtones of death. Othello's flaw is that he loves Desdemona blindly—that is, unrealistically; for that reason, Iago knows that such a naive man as Othello who loves his wife so blindly and unrealistically can be corrupted; in Act II, Scene 3, in one of his most villainous soliloquies, Iago speaks of Othello's relationship with Desdemona and joyously proclaims that Othello's "soul is so enfetter'd to her love/ That she may make, unmake, do what she list,/ Even as her appetite shall play the god/ With his weak function" (351-54). Iago is absolutely determined to pervert this man who has declared that he will deny his wife *nothing*; Iago is contemptuously certain that Othello can be corrupted simply because of his idealistic love for Desdemona.

Some critics think, of course, that Othello is sharply teasing with Desdemona (by calling her, at one point, "Desdemon"), but when one rereads more of the "deny thee nothing" quotation (III.iii.76), one realizes that Othello is clearly not teasing; this vow occurs with the lovely prelude of his calling her "sweet Desdemon." In addition, he also calls her "thee" and "sweet." And only moments later, he reveals even more clearly his love for Desdemona, his child-wife: "Excellent wretch!" he calls her, and says, "Perdition catch my soul/ But I do love thee! and when I love thee not,/ Chaos is come again" (90-92). There is tragic irony, of course, in this key speech; certainly the lines are full of portent, for order and calm are important ingredients of Othello's military life – until lately. Now he is married, and his order and self-controlled calm depend upon his assurance of love from Desdemona.

Finally, one must deal with Othello's flaws and, of these, perhaps our most major concern is the fact that he is able to deceive himself: Othello believes that he is a man who judges by the facts. In the past, this may have been true, but after Iago has infected him with a jealousy that overpowers all reason, Othello is doomed. Even when Iago made his initial overtures suggesting Desdemona's infidelity, Othello was firmly convinced that he was not a man to be self-deceived. In Act III, Scene 3 (obviously, the key scene of this tragedy), Othello says, "I'll see before I'll doubt; when I doubt, prove;/ And on the proof, there is no more but this, –/Away at once with love or jealousy!" (190-92). Othello will find, tragically, that it is not as easy as he thinks to make a *choice* between love and jealousy – and, at the same time, *dispel* the emotion that is not chosen. Othello's love for Desdemona continues and creates ever-new deceptions until the final climactic murder is accomplished. And even as he kills Desdemona, after he has decided that she must die, he deceives himself that he is killing her as a *duty*, as it were, not as revenge. In his words, he kills her "else she'll betray more men" (V.ii.6). Even at the end, he does not realize his true motivation for the murder of the woman he loves.

Iago

Few of Shakespeare's creations have been subject to such wide discussion and divergent points of view as has Iago. The Romantic poet and critic Samuel Taylor Coleridge was one of the first to come up with an interpretation that has survived to this day; he believed that the key to Iago's character was "motiveless malignity." This seems to be a bit simplistic. Iago is supremely dedicated to revenge, and he certainly has ample motive for it. In addition, we cannot sum up his villainy so easily because we are continually fascinated by his superb mastery of concealing his true thoughts and motives. In addition, Iago is one of the most sardonically witty and egotistical men in all literature—despite his being one of literature's most evil men.

The primary motive for Iago's villainy occurs in the first scene of the play—that is, Iago's injured vanity. For years, Iago has been his general's "ancient," his ensign. This is an honorable rank. Historically, an ensign carried the company's banner—which he was never to desert. In battle, if the company's banner was threatened, all the soldiers had to fight to defend it and also its bearer. Thus, an ensign, by tradition and definition, had to be universally well liked, brave, and, above all, trusted. Iago superlatively meets all these requirements. However, the position of ensign simply does not carry the military prestige that the title of "lieutenant" does. And it was this position that Iago not only wanted, but expected to receive. The play opens just as Iago has been passed over for this promotion, and it seems to be a promotion that he was quite deserving of. Thus we have the motivation for his hatred toward Othello and his jealousy toward Cassio.

In order to disguise his deep disappointment and conceal his plans for revenge, Iago begins early in the play to reinforce his image as an honest, loyal soldier. In Act I, Scene 2, for example, in a bit of playful boasting, Iago says that "in the trade of war I have slain men,/ Yet do I hold it very stuff o' th' conscience/ To do no contriv'd murder. I lack iniquity . . ." (1-3). This is an outright lie, but he has just come onstage with Othello, and he is saying this for his general's benefit, posing as the rough and ready, good-hearted soldier. In the same speech, he alludes to having had the opportunity to kill Roderigo—a man who has said evil things about Othello: "Nine or ten times/ I'd thought to have yerk'd him here under the ribs" (4-5). Clearly to us, Iago is lying about what he would actually have done, yet he wants to show that he is a loyal man of action, but one who would not kill impulsively. This, he is sure, will appeal to Othello, a professional military man. It is precisely this sort of behavior which secures Iago's reputation for cool, controlled honesty.

Cassio, however, the man who gained the position which Iago so desired, is wary of Iago. The two men bear little respect for one another; Iago, to Cassio, is merely a soldier, and in a sense, Cassio is right: Iago is a soldier—of the old-school type. The soldier's song he sings is manly and rough; he seems to be a good soldier who enjoys a good drink with his fellow soldiers. In contrast, Cassio is a man who has studied warfare, but one who has had little actual military experience.

Yet Cassio is one of Iago's fellow soldiers, and so Iago must artfully disguise his utter contempt for him. This he does superbly when he is speaking with Othello and is asked about his feelings toward Cassio; Iago uses the strong language of a manly, straightforward, courageous soldier – and, at the same time, he lies throughout the entire speech, feigning loyalty to a fellow soldier and all the while implying that he is reluctantly withholding the *full* truth: "I had rather have this tongue cut from my mouth/ Than it should do offence to Michael Cassio" (I.ii.21-22). This sort of brusque honesty (or so it would seem to be honesty) impresses and convinces Othello that his ensign is a good and loyal soldier, a soldier so loyal that, in his general's words, he might perhaps "mince this matter" – meaning that perhaps Iago might be refraining from saying things too sordid for his general to hear.

Speaking only minutes later to Cassio himself, Iago does not "mince matters": he pompously taunts Othello's new lieutenant. He scolds Cassio, a man he has privately called a "bookish theoric," for being "too severe a moraler" (I.iii.301). In other words, Iago is bragging that true soldiers have to be "tough" and can't think too much about wounding someone in a brawl – which Cassio has just done. This is the manly bluntness of the martial man, and it is this soldierly, blunt "honesty" which makes Iago seem so true and loyal to Othello – especially in the "temptation scene" (III.iii). There, Iago says to his general, "Men should be what they seem;/ Or those that be not, would they might seem none!" (126-27). Tragically for Othello, this sort of speech, ironically delivered in many variations by his trusted ensign, seems to be the very essence of straightforwardness.

Straightforwardness is Iago's public hallmark. Early in the play, Othello commends Iago to the Duke of Venice as "my ancient;/ A man he is of honesty and trust" (I.iii.284-85). This reputation for soldierly honesty, to which deceit is absolutely foreign, is the major reason for his powerful control over Othello. And we should not forget that Othello entrusts even his young bride to Iago's care when Othello is sent to Cyprus. It has been said, perhaps lightly, but not without a good deal of truth, that Iago is the most intelligent person in this drama; his intellectuality, of course, is a completely misguided intellectuality, but it is Iago's keen intellectuality that enables him to control superbly the events of the play. In Act II, Scene 3, Cassio is duped by Iago's cunning as Iago comforts Cassio's drunken remorse and counsels him to speak to Desdemona and ask her to try and convince Othello to reinstate Cassio as his lieutenant. "You advise me well. . . . Goodnight, honest Iago" (332/340), answers Cassio; thus, Othello is not the only one capable of falling under Iago's spell. Even Cassio, when he is tipsy, is capable of being convinced of Iago's honesty and "helpfulness." And not only Cassio, but even Desdemona concurs in the prevailing opinion of Iago: ". . . that's an honest fellow" (III.iii.5), as does Lodovico in Act V, Scene 1, when he refers to Iago as ". . . a very valiant fellow" (52). And, parenthetically, one might profitably note at this point that Othello not only continually refers to Iago's honesty but also his *thoughtfulness*, for in the "temptation scene" he says, ". . . I know thou'rt full of love and honesty,/ And weigh'st thy words before thou giv'st them breath . . ." (118-19). It is maddening at times in this drama to realize that Iago manages to shake Othello's faith not only in Desdemona, but also in humanity – for Othello continually reassures himself of Iago's "honesty." In this same "temptation scene," Othello insists upon Iago's "exceeding honesty." Here, particularly, one can see the extent to which Iago's success in corrupting Othello depends on his reputation for honesty. And as an additional bit of information, one should realize that "honesty" in Elizabethan times often implied a critical, searching mind, in addition to the traditional definition of rectitude. Perhaps the most climactic example of Othello's great statement of faith in Iago, which has never really wavered, occurs in Act V, Scene 1. He says, "O brave Iago, honest and just,/ That hast such noble sense of thy friend's wrong [Cassio's alleged seduction of Desdemona]! Thou teachest me" (31-33). This, one of Othello's last statements, is tragic proof of Iago's superbly successful villainy.

It is possible that at the core of Iago's villainy is a basic cynicism about all humanity. Even though he has proven himself to be a good soldier for years, Iago actually sneers at duty and loyalty. He considers himself to be beyond trivial morality. In fact, he seems incapable, finally, of any moral feeling. This we learn in Act I, Scene 1, when he is speaking to Roderigo: he says, "I follow him [Othello] to serve my turn upon him. . . . You shall mark/ Many a duteous and knee-crooking knave . . ." (42-45). Iago sorely lacks self-esteem, and it is only with difficulty that he maintains as much of it as he does, and this is due to the very fact that he *is* cynical; yet he can certainly offer other people conventional advice on how to value themselves, as is evident in Act I, Scene 3: ". . . and since I could distinguish betwixt a benefit and an injury, I never found man that knew how to love himself. Ere I would say I would drown myself for the love of a guinea-hen, I would change my humanity with a baboon" (313-18). Even the encouragement here offered to Roderigo (not to kill himself because he cannot have Desdemona – and thereby deprive Iago of Roderigo's pocketbook of money) involves a deep cynicism toward loving others.

To give the villain some small due, however, one might note that when Iago is jesting with Desdemona (II.ii.), he reveals his cynicism about women with a certain wit and playfulness: "She that was ever fair and never proud, . . . She was a wight, if ever such wights were, – . . . To suckle fools and chronicle small beer" (149-61). Women, he is saying, are "creatures"; but "wight" implies more than just a creature – it carries the dual definition of ambiguously meaning that women can be fairies – or witches! In either case, Iago says, in saucy and droll language, women are fit only to raise children and keep household accounts. Desdemona, however, is no fool; remember that she is, after all, a senator's daughter; she parries Iago's wit superbly: "O most lame and impotent [!] conclusion" (162).

It is possible that Iago's wit – cynical though it is – saves him from being such a thoroughly hateful scoundrel for the entire duration of this play. In Act II, Scene 1, when Cassio is profusely welcoming Emilia's safe arrival in Cyprus (in true Florentine fashion with a kiss), Iago reacts with a salty quip: "Sir, would she give you so much of her lips/ As of her tongue she oft bestows on me,/ You'd have enough" (101-3). This is exactly the kind of wit which gives Iago just enough of a satiric dimension to save him from being a pasteboard villain and, equally, this is proof of why others find him engaging. Yet one must never forget that beneath this wit there is a greedy jealousy toward this young and handsome Florentine who is kissing, if innocently, Iago's wife.

Iago's jealousy of Emilia is part and parcel of his attitude toward all women. Again, in this same scene, a few lines later, he says waggishly that women are "pictures out of door, . . . and housewives in your beds. . . . You rise to play, and go to bed to work" (110-16). He is pretending to clown here, but we are aware of a nearly psychotic conviction on his part about women's lustful natures; to him, they are little more than domestic whores.

This excessive bawdiness of Iago's is found throughout the play, beginning as early as Act I, Scene 1, when he urges Roderigo to inflame Desdemona's father with hatred for Othello. "Make after him," he says, meaning Brabantio, "poison his delight, Proclaim him in the streets. Incense her kinsmen,/ And, though he in a fertile climate dwell,/ Plague him with flies" (68-71). This is coarse language, indicating a certain blindness to all but the grosser emotions. When Iago fears that Roderigo may be too timid to arouse Brabantio's ire, Iago himself proclaims that Desdemona is a white ewe being "tupped" (mounted) by a black ram, meaning the Moor, Othello. Love, for Iago, scarcely exists, if at all. He sees only the sexual side of Othello and Desdemona's marriage; he is blind to their real romantic love for one another, as he reveals in Act II, Scene 1, when he talks with Roderigo and tries to convince him of the "violence" of Desdemona's initial "love" for the Moor. That "love," he assures Roderigo, will soon vanish, and Desdemona will "begin to heave the gorge, disrelish and abhor the Moor" (235-36). The language is shockingly savage. Yet to his general, to Othello, Iago's venomous language can be even more nakedly feral. Exciting Othello's imagination, he says in the "temptation scene" words that are potently effective: "Would you, . . . behold her topp'd?" (395-96). He asks Othello to envision the handsome Cassio ravishing Othello's young bride. In this entire scene, Iago knows, instinctively, the kind of remark that will increase Othello's suspicion without giving the impression that he wishes to do so. He asks Othello, for example, not to make him (Iago) strain his speech ". . . to larger reach/ Than to suspicion" (III.iii.218-19).

Yet, when all is said and done, Iago fascinates us. And perhaps this is true because great evil can somehow hold one—powerfully. Certainly, it is a tribute to Shakespeare's genius that despite everything evil which Iago accomplishes, the playwright never lets us forget that Iago *is* a human being, not an abstraction. Iago's jealousy is akin to jealousies we have had—except that he is *wildly* jealous; his passion is ours, except that he is immoral, ruthless, and savage; like Iago, our egos also succumb to envy and spite, but Iago cannot control an insatiable need to gratify his disappointments with revenge that is criminal. Iago has a satanic strain in him; he is devoid of all integrity. He is a clever, calculating madman, utterly unable to face the reality of his own nature or grasp the immensity of the chaos which he is responsible for. He finally becomes so poisoned by his own destructive power that he realizes that he too is lost, a victim in the very plot he so carefully and malignantly designed.

QUESTIONS FOR REVIEW

1. What does Roderigo hope to gain from Iago? Why is he paying him large amounts of money?

2. What is Iago's military position?

3. Why does Iago slip away so quickly after he and Roderigo have alerted Brabantio that Desdemona has eloped?

4. How does Othello defend himself to the Duke of Venice against Brabantio's accusations of witchcraft?

5. Describe Desdemona's defense of herself in choosing Othello as her husband.

6. Relate the details of Othello's arrival in Cyprus.

7. Comment on Iago's suspicions that not only Cassio, but also Othello, has had an affair with Emilia.

8. Explain Cassio's becoming drunk – despite the fact that he knows that he is not a "good drinker"; what does Iago hope to accomplish by having Roderigo and Cassio quarrel?

9. Paraphrase Iago's thoughts on the importance of one's reputation (when he is consoling the remorseful Cassio).

10. In your opinion, does Desdemona plead with Othello too often about his reinstating Cassio? Explain.

11. Describe Iago's first successes in making Othello believe that Desdemona and Cassio are lovers.

12. Does Iago ever say – outright – that Desdemona is unfaithful? If so, when?

13. What does the phrase "green-ey'd monster" refer to?

14. Describe the physical appearance of the handkerchief that Desdemona uses to try to soothe her irritated husband's brow; what is the history of the handkerchief?

15. Relate the details of Cassio's so-called "vocal" and "physical" dream that Iago says he witnessed while the two men spent the night together.

16. What scene in this drama is often referred to as the "temptation scene"?

17. At what point does Othello make Iago his new lieutenant?

18. Among Iago's many tricks to make Othello jealous, he refers to Desdemona's being typical of Venetian women; what does he mean by this?

19. In your opinion, why do so many people – Othello, in particular – refer to Emilia's husband as "honest Iago"?

20. Describe the scene that Iago arranges so that Othello can overhear Cassio speaking of his conquest of Bianca. How does Iago manage to convince Othello that Cassio is speaking about Desdemona?

21. Of all the ways that Othello considers murdering Desdemona, why does he finally decide to murder her in her bed?

22. Describe Lodovico's reaction when he arrives at Cyprus and sees his old friend Othello and his new bride together.

23. Explain Desdemona's summoning Iago – immediately after Othello has called her a whore and a strumpet; how does she hope to have Iago help her?

24. Describe Iago's plot to murder Cassio.

25. What elements in the "Willow Song" parallel Desdemona's own situation?

26. How is Roderigo killed?

27. What one last act does Othello perform before he murders Desdemona that is proof of his love and his regret for what he is about to do?

28. Why does Desdemona, with her dying breath, lie about Othello's guilt?

29. How does Othello die?

30. In this play, Othello is torn by a terrible dilemma – whether he can trust his new bride or whether he can trust his ensign. Why does he choose to trust the latter?

SELECTED BIBLIOGRAPHY

ADAMS, J. Q. *A Life of William Shakespeare.* Boston: Houghton Mifflin Co., 1923.

ALEXANDER, PETER. *Shakespeare.* Oxford: Oxford University Press, 1964.

BEVINGTON, DAVID. *Shakespeare.* Arlington Heights, Ill.: A.H.M. Publications, 1978.

BLOOM, EDWARD A., ed. *Shakespeare 1564-1964.* Providence: Brown University Press, 1964.

BRADLEY, A. C. *Shakespearean Tragedy.* London: The Macmillan Co., 1904.

BRYANT, J. A. *"Othello," Hippolyta's View: Some Christian Aspects of Shakespeare's Plays.* Lexington, Kentucky: University of Kentucky Press, 1961.

CAMPBELL, LILY B. *"Othello:* A Tragedy of Jealousy," *Shakespeare's Tragic Heroes.* Cambridge, England: Cambridge University Press, 1930.

_____. *Slaves of Passion.* New York: Barnes & Noble, Inc., 1959.

CHARLTON, H. B. *Shakespearean Tragedy.* Cambridge, England: Cambridge University Press, 1948.

CLEMEN, WOLFGANG. *"Othello," The Development of Shakespeare's Imagery.* Cambridge, Mass.: Harvard University Press, 1951.

CRAIG, HARDIN. "The Great Trio," *An Interpretation of Shakespeare.* Columbia, Missouri: Lucas Brothers, 1966.

FARNHAM, WILLARD. *The Medieval Heritage of Elizabethan Tragedy.* Berkeley, California: University of California Press, 1936.

GERARD, ALBERT. " 'Egregiously an Ass': The Dark Side of the Moor; A View of Othello's Mind," *Shakespeare Survey,* 10 (1957).

GIBSON, H. N. *The Shakespeare Claimants.* New York: Barnes & Noble, Inc., 1962.

GRANVILLE-BARKER, HARLEY. *Prefaces to Shakespeare,* 4th series: *Othello.* London: Sidgewick and Jackson, Ltd., 1945.

HEILMAN, ROBERT B. *Magic in the Web.* Lexington, Kentucky: University of Kentucky Press, 1956.

JOHNSON, SAMUEL. *Johnson on Shakespeare,* ed. Walter Raleigh. London: Oxford University Press, 1908; reprinted 1949.

KNIGHT, G. WILSON. *The Wheel of Fire.* London: Oxford University Press, 1930.

KIRSCHBAUM, LEO. "The Modern Othello," *ELH, A Journal of English Literary History,* XI (1944).

KOKERITZ, HELGE. *Shakespeare's Names: A Pronouncing Dictionary.* New Haven: Yale University Press, 1959.

LEAVIS, F. R. *The Common Pursuit.* Harmondsworth, Middlesex: Penguin Books, Ltd., 1963.

MUIR, KENNETH. *"Othello," Shakespeare's Sources.* London: Methuen & Co., Ltd., 1957.

RIBNER, IRVING. *Patterns in Shakespearean Tragedy.* New York: Barnes & Noble, Inc., 1960.

ROSENBERG, MARVIN. *The Masks of Othello.* Berkeley and Los Angeles: University of California Press, 1961.

SEWELL, ARTHUR. *Character and Society in Shakespeare.* Oxford: Clarendon Press, 1951.

SIEGEL, PAUL N. *"Othello," Shakespearean Tragedy and the Elizabethan Compromise.* New York: New York University Press, 1957.

SPIVACK, BERNARD. *Shakespeare and the Allegory of Evil.* New York: Columbia University Press, 1958.

SPRAGUE, ARTHUR COLBY. *"Othello," Shakespeare and the Actors.* Cambridge, Mass.: Harvard University Press, 1944.

WILSON, HAROLD S. *"Othello," On the Design of Shakespearean Tragedy.* Toronto: University of Toronto Press, 1957.

NOTES

NOTES

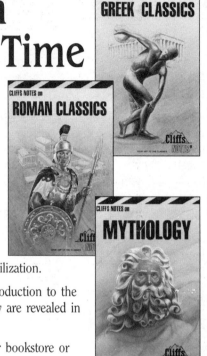

Your Guides to Successful Test Preparation.

Cliffs Test Preparation Guides

Efficient preparation means better test scores. Go with the experts and use **Cliffs Test Preparation Guides.** They'll help you reach your goals because they're: Complete • Concise • Functional • In-depth. They are focused on helping you know what to expect from each test. The test-taking techniques have been proven in classroom programs nationwide.

Recommended for individual use or as a part of formal test preparation programs.

NOTES